Jaime Osorio & Cristobal Reyes

Labour Super-Exploitation, Unequal Exchange, and Capital Reproduction

Writings on Marxist Dependency Theory

With a foreword by Andy Higginbottom

CRITICAL STUDIES ON LATIN AMERICA
DEBATES AND ALTERNATIVES FOR SOCIAL CHANGE

Edited by Mariano Féliz

Jaime Osorio & Cristobal Reyes

LABOUR SUPER-EXPLOITATION, UNEQUAL EXCHANGE, AND CAPITAL REPRODUCTION

Writings on Marxist Dependency Theory

With a foreword by Andy Higginbottom

Bibliographic information published by the Deutsche Nationalbibliothek
Die Deutsche Nationalbibliothek lists this publication in the Deutsche Nationalbibliografie; detailed bibliographic data are available in the Internet at http://dnb.d-nb.de.

Bibliografische Information der Deutschen Nationalbibliothek
Die Deutsche Nationalbibliothek verzeichnet diese Publikation in der Deutschen Nationalbibliografie; detaillierte bibliografische Daten sind im Internet über http://dnb.d-nb.de abrufbar.

ISBN-13: 978-3-8382-1796-3
© *ibidem*-Verlag, Hannover • Stuttgart 2024
All rights reserved.

Printed in the United States of America

Contents

Note on translations

Chapters 1, 2 and 4 were translated by Andy Higginbottom. Chapter 3 was translated by Cristóbal Reyes and revised by Ana Ortega.

The authors sincerely thank Andy Higginbottom for his generous support with the translations.

Foreword

I am pleased and honoured to write a short foreword to this work. The authors' Introduction that immediately follows gives an excellent presentation to this collection of essays. In this light, I strongly recommend studying Marini's *The Dialectics of Dependency* in conjunction with the present work. Ruy Mauro Marini initiated the trend of revolutionary thought known as Marxist dependency theory, that is here taken forward and developed in a most appropriate and timely manner. Thanks to Amanda Latimer's determined efforts in cooperation with Jaime Osorio, *Dialectics* is now available in English after an extraordinary delay.[1]

Dependency theory emerged in the 1950s as a broad current of consciousness protesting against the framing of Latin America as a "backward" and "less developed" region. The dependency theory critics pointed out the effects of three hundred years and more of colonialism, then the informal empire of free trade in the nineteenth century that was *de facto* dominated by Britain, and then again the domination of US imperialism in the twentieth century all involved the transfer of wealth out of Latin America to enrichen the empires of the North. They argued that Latin America had been and continues to be poor because precisely as it enriches the imperialist countries, it is trapped in exploitative international relations that impoverish it, and that it needs to break free from if its peoples are ever to truly develop.

As you will go on to read in this volume, the specifically Marxist trend within the dependency tradition concentrated analysis on the class realities of capitalist underdevelopment; polarised internally between ruling classes that are dependent on imperialism and hence structurally incapable of breaking from its demands, and working classes whose lives are cursed by exhausting overwork, brutal conditions and low pay that Marini

---

1   For those who wish to explore them, due to the efforts of the current authors, Marini's entire works and other related materials are available in Spanish at the website https://marini-escritos.unam.mx.

encapsulated as *labour super-exploitation*. Developing from this central category that took Marxism beyond Marx, Marini explained all the main features that characterise the internal political economy of Latin America, and related them to the mode of its subordinate insertion in the world economy. The political implication was clearly for revolution and socialism, rather than reforms and the false promise of another version of capitalism.

Of course, vigorous debates ensued on the Latin American left, and did so in the face of horrific US backed coups that rained down as drastic preventative measures against the spread of the Cuban revolution. In the meantime, some reformist and even radical texts of dependency theory found their way into the English language. They were generally critiqued by orthodox Marxists in comprehensive terms: for being weak in their understanding of Marx's categories such as surplus value; for substituting nation for class; for forgetting the centrality of class struggle and promoting alliances with the national bourgeoisie; and so on. In my view these critics were more influenced by Eurocentric prejudices than by Marxism. Rather than picking over the weaker points of the dependency arguments, the critics should have been more generous and looked for the strong point of even the less than perfect dependency works available to them, which in its essence was a denunciation of imperialism. But, more importantly, the main works of Marini and other coherent writers from the Marxist current of dependency were simply not translated into English. With very few honourable exceptions there was little effort to meet up with and engage constructively with this highly significant current of thought, let alone (heaven forbid!) learn from its conceptual advance. The epistemological exclusion of Marini and the revolutionary wing of dependency theory is only now, some fifty years later, being overcome.

This then is the background against which I see the current volume as a welcome addition to the growing literature of Marxist dependency theory available in English. Now to the authors and the work itself.

Our first author Jaime Osorio is an esteemed professor, resident in Mexico where he fled in exile from the Pinochet dictatorship in Chile. Osorio was a student, then comrade and personal friend of Marini. For several years I have followed Osorio's work as the most knowledgeable and principled current defender of Marini's legacy in contemporary debates. He has written a series of books and articles that in my view are exemplary in their conceptual clarity and conviction. I am also heartened that he is co-authored by Cristóbal Reyes, a young Mexican scholar who has joined forces with Jaime in a productive collaboration that carries forward into the next generation.

The Introduction and the first essay emphasise the specificity of Latin America in its relations with the capitalist world system. I want to support this point from my own studies and experience. There is no doubt of the authentic grounding of Marxist dependency theory in Latin American realities. The veins of Latin America are still open. In my travels and researches, mostly in Colombia and then elsewhere in the Andean region, I have found a fundamental confirmation of the Marxist dependency approach in the common sense of social movements in struggle, especially those confronting violent extractivism. International capital, that is multinational corporations exploiting oil, mining, forests and fisheries work through alliances with domestic bourgeois class holding state power. This syndrome of neo-colonial dependency is more present in the smaller economies of the Andean region and Central America. Even when it comes to Latin America's two biggest countries, Brazil and Mexico, where there has been more space opened up for the growth of domestic industrialisation and indeed stronger national capitals, even so these economies are still held as subordinate in the international division of labour by a web of external constraints and processes.

Osorio's contributions are important because they lay out the position of Latin America in the capitalist world system from a revolutionary class perspective. This is complemented by Reyes' extended literature review that probes more specifically into the political economy of international trade.

Reyes looks anew at the long running problem called "unequal exchange", the syndrome in international trade where the labour producing commodities in the global South counts for less money in the markets than does commodity producing labour in the global North. He reviews the relevant literature on this topic over three theoretical generations. This endeavour has huge significance as a critique of the world capitalist system, not least for understanding the political economic contradictions driving US aggression towards China for instance. Starting with the first generation, in *Capital* Marx provides important insights, if not a definitive explanation of international trade– primarily his comments on national differences in wages, Chapter 22 of Volume 1; and the transformation of values into prices, the first two parts of Volume 3, an issue we will come back to shortly. The next generation is the classical Marxist theories of imperialism whose most renowned authors (Hilferding, Luxemburg, Bukharin, Lenin) wrote in the immediate antecedents or during the 1914-18 war. The main work of Henryk Grossman was published in Germany in 1929 and recently republished in English in a new translation as *The Law of Accumulation and Breakdown of the Capitalist System: Being also a Theory of Crises*. It should be read in conjunction with these better known "big four", for he shares their objective to apply Marx's mature theory to analysing capitalism as modern imperialism. Unsurprisingly given his timing and location, Grossman is above all concerned to explain capitalism's inherent tendency to breakdown, which he does by outlining connections between falling profitability with imperialism and crises, that inevitably lead to assaults on the working class.

Reyes addresses how the next theoretical generation applied to international trade another of Marx's core theories, the transformation of commodity values into prices of production. The main discussion occurred in the 1970s triggered by the book *Unequal Exchange: A Study of Imperialism of Trade* by Egyptian scholar Arghiri Emmanuel. Marx's treatment had set the condition of equalised profit rates for aggregate capitals of different industrial sectors, differentiated by their average organic composition of capital, that is the weight of capital invested in machinery and raw materials as compared to that invested in labour power; in short high-tech and low-tech sectors. Emmanuel was the first to introduce another variable into the transformation mix, different rates of surplus value by region, in the global North or South, as a second and for him more significant factor in unequal exchange. Emmanuel argued that radically different national

wage levels are the leading determinant of international prices of production, and therefore transfers of surplus-value. Reyes explores the counter
position argued by Bettelheim and other critics that gives primary emphasis to inequalities in the productive forces as the reason for surplus-value
transfer. This discussion is supremely important and will continue.

While the initial exchanges were mostly in the French language, the
debate was quickly picked up and developed in Latin America. Certainly,
Marini was well versed in this literature, that he pushed on further again
by situating labour super-exploitation as the underlying social relation of
unequal exchange, pivotal in the broader context of capitalist underdevelopment.

The approach initiated by Marini and developed by all the essays
here advances the Marxist paradigm in a qualitative way, in that it analyses
capitalist imperialism from the perspective of the oppressed and super-ex-
ploited working class in the subordinated countries of the Third World, or
Global South. Hence its relevance beyond the particular, as a vital contribution to the necessary updating of the classical Marxist theories of imperialism as a world system. Understanding unequal exchange as global value
transfers is at the root of the world capitalist system today, the source of its
new lease of life through the shift to off-shoring manufacturing industries,
and at the same time the form of renewed fundamental contradictions,
such the tensions between the US and China that look to dominate international relations for decades.

What then of the significance of this collection of essays? I believe it
is threefold a) it gives us a theoretically informed understanding of the mo-
tors of social change in Latin America, b) it surveys and evaluates the debate on unequal exchange by including a critical interrogation of how international trade reproduces underdevelopment. These points I have
briefly covered, but there is a c), this book alerts us to our own responsibilities as workers located on the more privileged other side of the world
system.

Let me illustrate the last point by turning to my contemporary context in the UK. As I write, the liberal, apparently "left of centre" *Guardian*
newspaper reports that its founders two hundred years ago were

Manchester cotton merchants and manufacturers, that is they were major beneficiaries of slavery in the US, as well as one backer who directly owned a sugar plantation in Jamaica 2. Shameful it certainly is, and *The Guardian* as an institution should make itself fully accountable. But if truth be told this relation between the profits of the industrial revolution and the violent racism of slavery has been evident for a long time, not least to the enslaved workers themselves in their rising up, as told by W.E. Du Bois in *Black Reconstruction in America*. In their time Marx and Engels condemned cotton slavery as one of the twin pillars of capitalism. Eric Williams' breakthrough study demonstrated how plantation slavery in the Caribbean stimulated manufacturing in Britain. Eric Hobsbawm explained how decades after slavery was abolished in the British empire, slave produced cotton remained the mainspring of British industry. Black scholarship and activism in the US have inspired a new generation of excellent historical studies that seek to foreground the lived experiences of enslavement, to imaginatively reconstruct what it was like. No shortage of evidence then. So, reporting that Manchester manufacturers profited from slavery as a major revelation is frankly a nonsense.

Why now *The Guardian* has acknowledged the origins of its wealth and standing, is because of the agency of black people, especially of the Black Lives Matter movement, has made this a necessary admission. The issue for them now is a managed damage limitation exercise to protect the paper's reputation.

The relevance of the current book is in developing a *strategic* and *categorical* critique of the system that has thrived on such brutal practices. This is not just institutional racism, it is the systemic racism of capitalism. This fits into a pattern that the champions of liberalism were at the same time leading imperialists, from Jeremy Bentham to J.S. Mill, from J.M. Keynes to one Tony Blair. Nor do we forget that as manufacturers they were the principal authors of exploitation at home as well, their cotton mills were mostly staffed by women, teenagers and children. I would say,

---

2   See https://www.theguardian.com/news/series/cotton-capital.

although *The Guardian* would doubtless not, that its founders profited from the racialised *super*-exploitation of enslaved Africans and African descendant Americans.

Slavery and colonial labour super-exploitation are the untold truths that have been outlawed by the hegemony of false historical narratives. Restoration of the truth against amnesia and denial, and the calls for apology and reparations, are justified in their own right. But it is not only the injustices of the past but those of the present that are of even greater concern as we think of ways to move forward.

Labour super-exploitation is all around today. A glimpse of this comes in another *Guardian* story, of strawberry pickers in the Huelva district in the south of Spain 3. The workers are immigrants from Africa on temporary stays up to nine months at time. They must not stay. It is their labour power that is wanted, not them. Women aged between 25 to 45 years are preferred, for it is assumed that they have children and hence are expected to return home when their work is done. The newspaper article is based on the Ethical Consumer report *Produce of Exploitation* that documents endemic "forced labour, union busting, unsafe working conditions, payment of less than minimum wage, excessive working hours, failure to provide regular employment, discrimination, including sexual harassment, harsh and inhumane treatment" in Huelva and neighbouring Almeria.

Authors writing from the perspective of Marxist dependency theory would see this as another example of labour super-exploitation, in that it demonstrates an even greater degree of exploitation than is normal for workers in Spain. The conditions endured by African women workers in Spain is an extension of even worse situations in Morocco and sub-Saharan Africa. "Cheap labour" practices are not marginal in today's world economy, on the contrary they have been the central motor of the global shift

---

3   Kassam, Ashifa and Brenda Chavez (2023), "Abusive working conditions endemic in Spain's strawberry farms, report claims", *The Guardian*, London, 31 March, https://www.theguardian.com/global-development/2023/mar/31/abusive-working-conditions-endemic-in-spains-strawberry-farms-report-claims.

in manufacturing production to the global South including of course China, that has taken place over the last generation. Labour super-exploitation is essential to capitalism as it operates at the global level.

This book is for those eager to go deeper into the matter and explore the structural reasons for continuing outrages. Marxist dependency theory clarifies and explains the processes of capitalist underdevelopment in Latin America, and with some qualifications, across Africa and Asia as the tricontinental, also known together as the Third World, the Global South or the Majority World.

Which brings us back to Osorio's essays, that I read as an appreciation of Marini's tremendous capacity to apply Marx's dialectical method to the particular realities confronted by workers in the global South. It is fitting that the collection ends with an explanation of the persistent tendency of the masses to revolution in Latin America. Despite the nightmare years of military dictatorship, disappearances and torture the movements managed to recover. Despite all the efforts at counter revolution and the harsh squeeze of the US embargo, liberated Cuba still survives intent on protecting the social gains of the 1959 Revolution. Despite over five centuries of plunder indigenous communities persevere in their resistance and defence of *Pachamama*. Despite their criminalisation by governments and state institutions working hand in hand with the multinationals, there have in the last few years been popular explosions, *estallidos sociales*, the length and breadth of the Andean region. Despite the compromises and mistakes of the first "Pink Tide", there is now a second tide, with social democratic governments seeking to resolve the enormous contradictions. And yet the robbing continues, by European capital as much as the US, with now Chinese corporations on the flanks as well. The mechanisms of unequal exchange explored in this book are multiplied by the haemorrhage of corporate profits and outflowing debt payments that weaken national currencies and once again threaten to crucify the continent.

Marxist dependency theory, and especially the concept of labour super-exploitation corresponds with the experiences of the more oppressed sections of the world working class. It positions their objective role in boosting capitalist profits. The oppressed workers of the world are where the principal agency for fundamental change comes from.

I hope that studying this volume will inspire responses and lead to deepening our international collaboration as an essential contribution to a better future than the current shambles that unfortunately pervades the socialist left almost as acutely as the multiple crises of capitalism.

These essays are an important contribution to a rejuvenated wave of Marxist dependency theory that has its purpose to not only understand the world but to change it. This literature is moving in the right direction, which is to create a mutual theoretical understanding of the workings of capitalist imperialism with a view to rebuilding workers solidarity integrally as an internationalist movement. To succeed we must overcome the divisions of imperialism wherever we can. The multiple crises that beset the world system are all expressions of the inner exhaustion yet recklessness of the capitalist mode of production. Matters are once again surely coming to a head.

Andy Higginbottom
London, 31 March 2023

Introduction

Marxist dependency theory is one of the main contributions of Latin American thought to the social sciences in general. This theory, whose initial stage of formulation took place between the 1960s and 1970s, explains the particularities of Latin America in the capitalist world system, as well as the main economic, political and social contradictions resulting from the reproduction of dependent capitalism. In this book, we present some of the fundamental theses of Marxist dependency theory and emphasise its relevance for the analysis of Latin American societies.

A crucial argument of Marxist dependency theory is that the so-called "underdevelopment" or "backwardness" of Latin America is not the result of a lack of maturity of capitalism. On the contrary, Latin America is a fully mature region in terms of the deployment of capital, and its characteristics are only intelligible within the framework of the dynamics and relations that organise capitalism as a world system. In this way, Marxist dependency theory opened a horizon of critical reflection to account for the particularities of capitalism in Latin America, which differs substantially from the analyses of the region proposed by mainstream academia and by international organisations.

The originality of capitalism in Latin America should therefore not be understood as immaturity or insufficiency. On the contrary, dependent capitalism is a specific, fully mature, *sui generis* form that capitalism assumes in its reproduction. Marxist dependency theory studies the main relations and processes that determine the heterogeneous deployment of capitalism as a world system and that define the particularities of Latin American dependent capitalism: the super-exploitation of labour-power, unequal exchange, the rupture in the cycle of capital, among others.

The core of this book's concerns is to explain the main processes that account for the specificity of Latin American capitalism, both in its internal reproduction and in its relation to the capitalist world system. The book is comprised of four essays, which present the classic contributions of

Marxist dependency theory and current debates on this perspective, highlighting its relevance for the study of contemporary processes in Latin America.

The first chapter offers a panoramic view of the history of Latin America and its most relevant political processes, linking them to the trajectory of Latin American social theory. After reviewing some of the main approaches to explain the particularities of the region, the specificity and analytical power of the formulations proposed by Marxist dependency theory on the *sui generis* character of capitalism in Latin America are highlighted. This chapter also contextualises the origin of Marxist dependency theory and underlines the political relevance of its formulations by considering the main political processes and the intellectual environment in which it emerged. Finally, the main arguments of Marxist dependency theory are presented to explain the specific ways in which the laws of capitalism have shaped Latin American dependent capitalism by commenting on the most relevant work of this theory—Ruy Mauro Marini's *The Dialectics of Dependency*—and its influence on the Latin American debate.

Chapter 2 discusses the fundamentals of labour super-exploitation, which is considered by Marxist dependency theory as the foundation of dependent capitalism. This chapter points out why labour super-exploitation —a concept that refers to refers to the violation of the value of labour-power—is necessary in the dynamics of dependent capitalism. Starting from pointing out the determinations of the value of labour-power, this chapter discusses the different forms of labour super-exploitation. While the payment of wages below the value of labour-power also occurs in developed capitalism, especially in periods of crisis, in dependent capitalism labour super-exploitation assumes particular forms and operates as a systematic and regular process. The consequences of labour super-exploitation extend to the whole of dependent capitalism—determining particular forms of production, circulation, distribution and consumption—which is why it gives rise to a qualitatively different form of reproduction of capital.

The third chapter, written by Cristóbal Reyes, presents a broad review of the Marxist debate on "unequal exchange" as a means through which the unevenness of capitalism as a world system is reproduced. The chapter begins with a reconstruction of Marx's main arguments on foreign trade and on the determinations of unequal exchange. Subsequently, a detailed review is made of the formulations of the main Marxist authors of the 20th century on unequal exchange. Finally, the contributions of Marxist dependency theory to the understanding of unequal exchange are highlighted, and the implications of this process for the reproduction of Latin American dependent capitalism are analysed. It is concluded that unequal exchange is one of the fundamental determinations of dependent capitalism because it gives rise to differentiated conditions of value appropriation in the world system and, consequently, it determines qualitatively different forms of capital reproduction between dependent and imperialist countries.

Lastly, chapter 4 links the main characteristics of dependent capitalism—in particular, labour super-exploitation and the rupture in the cycle of capital—with its most significant social and political implications. In dependent countries, the systemic contradictions of capitalism are condensed, and the resulting conflicts are exacerbated. As a result, Latin America constitutes—to borrow Lenin's expression—a "weak link" in the imperialist chain: a space where social irruptions and tendencies of rupture that question the domination of capital are persistently present. This is why throughout the history of capitalism and in recent periods the possibility of revolution and the most significant social rebellions have been particularly present in dependent capitalism, not in the imperialist countries.

Despite its relevance, Latin American Marxist dependency theory is little known to English-language readers. With this book, we hope to contribute to the wider dissemination of this fundamental contribution of Latin American social theory to the understanding of the relations of domination and dependency in the world system, as well as on the contradictions of capitalism in Latin America.

The authors

The Latin American Question[4]

I

Latin America maintains a conflictive place within the universal discourse built by capitalist modernity. At the heart of this great narrative, the region and its processes appear as a remnant that questions and denies that universality. This requires new thinking that explains the reasons for such denial.

II

Capitalist modernity—at different times and in the voices of diverse authors and trends—formed a narrative of powerful intellectual and political force. It offered multiple civilising promises of comprehensive humanisation of development and prosperity for the people, of a state order founded in liberties that would reconcile individual and social interests, and of political and social equalities. From its inclusion in the universal history that constructed capital, the region that would later be called Latin America emerged as a necessary exclusion (therefore its inclusion) that makes modernity viable. The imperial centres were abundant in their grand political revolutions, powerful industrial transformations, productive ebullience and progress, and everything related to humanity and well-being that is produced there. But this had its counterpart in colonialism: pillaging, plundering of riches, and the extermination of indigenous peoples, the montage of a colonial organization of subjugation and the forced dispossession of land that also required the destruction of numerous African peoples who were transported as slaves to the plantations and mines of the region, and subjugated to inhumane conditions that caused thousands of deaths.

---

4   This chapter is based on "The Latin American Debate: Dependent Capitalism, Superexploitation, and Revolution", *Social Justice*, vol. 40, n. 4, 2014, pp. 5-24.

Marx (1976: 926) was not using a mere metaphor when he pointed out that capitalism comes into the world "dripping from head to toe, from every pore, with blood and dirt." Capitalism was established in the new European society, where its novel form of organisation was crystallised, but it was also present, with a degree of unusual brutality, in the colonial world and, with all the more reason, in Latin America and the Caribbean, which played a central role in this history.

III

Revolutions and Counter-Revolutions in Our History

Relevant milestones in the mid-20th century indicate the undeniable cracks that pierce capitalist modernity: two world wars, severe economic crises, proletarian revolutions, the Holocaust, atomic explosions over Japanese territory, among others. For the dominant discourse, these excesses are explained in different ways from outside of the logic of capital.

By the mid-20th century, Latin America already had a history of significant popular revolutions and uprisings. Add to these an eruption of revolutions without any established institutionality, in particular the Cuban Revolution. In the midst of a world divided by the Cold War and situated only a few miles from the system's imperialist centre, the Cuban Revolution caused commotion and readjustments not only at the central of power but in the entire region. This genuine "assault of reality" revealed an obscene nucleus throughout the region's history, with nearly permanent systemic and regional trends of energetic rupture that would persist in diverse forms and degrees. The Revolution occurred nearly 150 years after the constitution of formally independent nations, yet regional history still presented serious difficulties for generating processes that would combine growth and well-being (Fajnzylber, 1989). On the contrary, poverty, backwardness, and inequity were common terms used to describe the prevailing conditions for most of the population. These political and economic processes raise the same reasonable question: why is it that in Latin America growth processes do not elevate well-being among most of the population and therefore encourage tendencies of rupture and revolution? The debates about the Latin American way of being, as well as the projects and practices that would be set into motion as a response, mark the second half of the 20th century and into the 21st century.

IV

Along with its singular meaning, from a broad historical perspective the Cuban Revolution updated Latin America's particularity as a region of systemic contradictions that question and fracture the dominant order. In this sense, it is related to at least two previous revolutions that were just as surprising: that of Saint-Domingue (now Haiti) of 1791-1805, which was the first in this part of the world to be organized by slaves and which also led to independence and the end of slavery. Then the Mexican Revolution of 1910-1914 opened the worldwide revolutionary cycle of the 20th century—which Hobsbawm (2012) calls the short century—that ended with the defeat of socialism in 1989. If the slaves' revolution of Haiti made evident the processes of negation that maintained and enabled the French Revolution's universal mottos of liberty, equality, and fraternity,5 Mexico's peasant revolution preceded the first triumphant worker-peasant revolution, which was that of the Soviets, the Bolsheviks, and Vladimir Lenin, and shows a tendency in the progression of those processes: revolutions tended to implode within the capitalist periphery.

The West Indian colonies generally contributed to their respective empires with great flows of commodities, such as sugar, coffee, and tobacco. Haiti was by far the richest colony, with plantations that were organized under the strict demands of capitalist rationalization (Grüner, 2007: 84). And the slaves of the great plantations on the northern part of the island (those most subjected to that rationality) were the main actors in the unexpected black revolution (Feijoo, 2010). Faced with the French Revolution's fractured universalism ("we are all equal") while the centre nevertheless accepted the benefits of exploiting slaves in the colonies, the Haitian

---

5   As Louis Sala-Molins states, "European Enlightenment philosophers railed against slavery, except where it literally existed" (cited by Zizek, 2009: 111).

Constitution of 1805 proclaimed that "all Haitian citizens are Black" which beyond skin colour contrasted sharply with the many that were not accounted for in the French Revolution's claim to speak for "all" (Grüner, 2009: 83). Therefore, as Zizek emphasizes, "the point is not to study the Haitian Revolution as an extension of the European revolutionary spirit ... but rather to assert the significance of the Haitian Revolution for Europe. It is not only that one cannot understand Haiti without Europe—one cannot understand either the scope or the limitations of the European emancipation process without Haiti" (2009: 121).

Without causing a radical shift in the relationships of power between the ruling class and its subjects, the Mexican Revolution brought about a deep change in the ruling political regime. Those who were "nonexistent" in the eyes of the oligarchic power 6—the peasants, miners, agricultural and urban workers, and poor people in general—burst open the reigning order and established their place. True, their corporatist designation was subordinated to the command of pacts of loyalty based on political foundations inherited from the viceroyalty of New Spain, as opposed to the ideals of the citizens and conditions of the rule of law under liberal representative democracy (González Callejas, 2011). However, we should not lose sight of the rupture in oligarchic relationships or of the achievements gained in community recognition, the restitution of territories and land rights, and of multiple social rights for extensive sectors of the population in the midst of new reconfigurations of power and control. Indigenous peasants and agricultural workers from the haciendas protested and created rebel armies in response to the growing process of expropriation of community and peoples' lands by landowners. They also reacted against the miserable conditions to which workers were condemned (in the mines, railways, and other services) to increase profits under the 19th century

---

6   In Alain Badiou's terms: "In Marx's analysis of bourgeois or capitalist societies, the proletariat is truly the non-existent characteristic of political multiplicities. It is 'that which does not exist.' That does not mean that it has no being.... The social and economic being of the proletariat is not in doubt. What is in doubt, always has been, and is now so more than ever, is its political existence" (Badiou, 2010: 130-131).

export model. It was the lack of moderation inherent in capitalist profit that led to the revolutions in Mexico and Haiti.

To emphasize, as much as land dispossessions, it was the pursuit of profit that gave meaning to the pre-capitalist forms operating in the large Mexican haciendas during the *porfiriato* period (rule by Porfirio Díaz from 1876 to 1911). And it was capitalist logic that organised the exploitation of slaves on the Haitian plantations. This fact allows us to understand that these revolutions—regardless of their social majorities (slaves in one case, peasants in the other) and the directions they took—were responding to the operations of capital, embodied in slave-owning exporters, mine owners, and landowners, all of whom were trapped in the logic of profit. Despite being fed by capital, they are not anti-capitalist revolutions. Both revolutions demanded land distribution and the establishment of small agricultural properties as a central objective. Yet, this is not to minimize the unthinkable event that both represent in history.

A century separates the revolutions in Haiti and Mexico, with half a century separating the latter from the Cuban Revolution. That second period represents 50 years of global maturity of worldwide capitalism, and of the maturation of regional and Cuban capitalism in particular. The commotion resulting from the 26th of July Movement's overthrow of a US-sponsored dictatorship on the biggest island in the Caribbean is followed by another, no less relevant event, when the Cuban Revolution proclaimed itself a socialist revolution in 1961. A project defining itself as anti-capitalist took form and its power was consolidated in the region.

Fuelled by the fervour and ebullience unleashed by the Cuban feat, Latin American political organisations arose in the 1970s that took up the revolutionary mantle and set out to reissue or re-create the great deeds of Fidel and Che. Beyond the voluntarism and the utopianism of many of these processes, their multiplication and expansion were favoured by prevailing political and economic conditions. The abysmal living conditions of most of the population continued as authoritarian governments multiplied and wealth remained in the hands of very few. At this point, Washington demanded reforms from governments in the region, such as land redistribution and a greater level of industrialization, while agreeing to the creation and preparation of counterinsurgent military squads capable of containing the pressure cooker.

V

Experiencing the antithesis of the Cuban experience would bring to light the region's impulse toward rupture during this period. In Chile in 1970, Salvador Allende the leftist candidate for President triumphed after four previous electoral defeats. After a few disputed elections, the parties representing the dominant sectors were divided, making it possible for an alliance of the declaredly Marxist Communist and the Socialist parties to predominate. With 33 percent of the votes, Allende was proclaimed President of the Chilean Republic, thus opening the door to a revolutionary process that profoundly affected society and, as an exceptional process, surprised insiders and outsiders alike. What followed was unique in history and established some of the Gordian knots of that experience. The combination of a popular government enclave embedded within the state apparatus and the intention to transform society without abandoning the prevailing institutionality became a formula known as the "Chilean road to socialism." Dozens of important factories passed into state hands and remained under the management of the workers. The great copper deposits, once in the hands of important US firms, were nationalized. In the factories, country estates, schools and towns, peasants, urban workers, students, and townspeople began discussions and took greater responsibility for the country's productive and political life. Within a few months, the country and society became mobilised, constantly organising and reorganising, and the level of politicisation grew. Society became increasingly polarised politically. Allende and his allies gained strength in the Congress with triumphs in parliamentary elections, thus opening institutional routes to economic transformations, such as the nationalisation of copper, state-controlled businesses, and land redistribution. Meanwhile, the political forces of capital obstructed change by entrenching themselves in the institutions of the state apparatus they still controlled, such as the judicial branch and some quarters of the legislative branch, while business sectors unhinged the economy by generating shortages and a black market. They mobilised their social sectors in street demonstrations, such as the *cacerolazos* (pots and pans protests), and organized paramilitary forces. At the same time, they manoeuvred within the Armed Forces and the *carabineros* (armed police) to disrupt the institutional order, fearing that the popular sectors would continue to gain strength in a setting in which they caused tension while respecting the law.

After a few failed coup attempts, the "Chilean road to socialism" was violently shut down in September 1973, after a military coup supported by most of the high command of the Armed Forces and Police. Thus began a long and bloody counterrevolutionary process. The military coup high-lighted the enormous tactical flexibility of the dominant groups in main-taining their power. If respect for the law and their institutionality were not sufficient instruments for confronting the popular offensive, then the problem had to be resolved in the arena of concentrated violence, thus vi-olating their own armed apparatuses of the state, the law, and the Consti-tution. The bombing at La Moneda Palace by Air Force warplanes, and the death of President Allende while defending the Constitution in a building surrounded by the coup leaders' troops, are vivid images of the contradic-tions marking that process.

VI

After successive military coups in the southern part of the continent, the wave of insurgency that traversed the region arrived to Central America, taking form in the triumph of the Sandinista Revolution of 1979 and in intense civil wars in El Salvador and Guatemala in the 1980s. These pro-cesses culminated in electoral and/or military defeats, accompanied by se-rious processes of political decomposition. This closed the cycle initiated with the Cuban Revolution. The counterrevolutionary period took full form with the 1964 military coup in Brazil. By the 1970s, almost all of the countries in the South American region of Latin America came under the rule of military dictatorships—a trend that travelled north into a large part of Central America in the 1980s.

The new dictatorships were not merely a reactive response to popular offensives. For the most part, they imposed new projects of economic and political reorganisation, or cleared the way for civil governments to undertake that task. During the 1970s and 1980s, the region was reinserted into the world market in the form of specialized exports and neoliberal economic policies. The common denominator in this intense process of productive restructuring was an aggressive policy against the working classes, with wages and social benefits plummeting. The monopolistic sector of local capital and the sector more closely associated with foreign capital were strengthened. This process was fuelled by the privatisation of important state businesses, the narrowing of trade relations, and opening up to the world market. Increased competitiveness in foreign markets was closely bound to deteriorating living conditions for waged employees and to intensified exploitation. Not surprisingly, the region's export capacity grew during the last decades of the 20th century, while wages plummeted. The economy turned its back on most of the working population, and after a brief period of industrialising in the region, the working population was partly incorporated into the internal market.

VII

Once the foundations of the new economic organisation were in place, with its corresponding disciplining of the working population, and once the most intense phases of the crisis had been dealt with, it became possible to retire the military regimes and the authoritarian civilians as part of a region-wide agenda. This was fuelled by US think tanks under the theme of "transition to democracy" (Huntington, 1991). Political leaders were granted new levels of legitimacy within a framework fully compatible with the prevailing neo-liberalism. "Obese" states—those packed with public businesses that granted social benefits and sustained broad class alliances—were replaced by "efficient" states that concentrated on safeguarding the local and transnational interests of big capital in the region. A new figure of the citizen made their entrance as one who received fair pay from the market for their efforts and capacities, replacing the subject who waited for hand-outs and state benefits. Authorities would be elected by the votes of political adults, now enjoying access to a public life, thus leaving behind the idea of masses manipulated by *caudillos* (populist, authoritarian leaders) and tropical strongmen.

Three decades after the transition to democracy began in the region and the consequent "democratic consolidation" called for by this theoretical agenda, the results fell short of the expectations of the dominant and popular sectors alike. For the former, democracy has brought about serious disappointments because of the emergence of leaders elected by the masses, such as Hugo Chávez in Venezuela and Evo Morales in Bolivia. This was also due to the increase in social disturbances (or downright chaos in some cases, such as Mexico and Guatemala), and even to the emergence of social movements in societies that were orderly not so long before, as occurred in Chile in 2011, with thousands of high school and university students disturbing social peace. From the perspective of the dominant sectors, however, the pros outweigh the cons. The great regional capitalist transformation that accompanied globalisation gave the region an almost unequalled dynamism, as well as a growing presence in global politics. Brazil, Argentina, and Mexico joined the G-20, and the importance of their exports, purchases, and investments, particularly in the case of Brazil, represents revitalising factors for the regional and world economies.

From the perspective of the popular sectors, the transition to democracy has not achieved its promise. Aside from Bolivia, Venezuela, and Ecuador, despite voting for and electing politicians who promised change, they have experienced an inability to modify ruling neoliberal guidelines alongside deteriorating living conditions. No mechanism exists for them to demand accountability from elected administrations, much less to revoke their terms in office. Electoral fraud is compounded by job insecurity, a lack of employment, at times an even greater military presence in the streets and on highways, as well as higher levels of insecurity. Some sectors increasingly believe and state in diverse ways that this form of democracy offers little as a mechanism for broadening the capacity of many to determine the direction of their community life. In the words of Mexican film director Alfonso Cuaron, "the tyranny happening now is taking on new disguises—the tyranny of the 21st century is called 'democracy'" (quoted in Zizek, 2009b: 24). For many who represent quite divergent positions, enthusiasm for the prevailing democracy has been waning. So, think tanks representing a wide array of political perspectives have assumed the task of shoring it up. The common denominator in debates in the region is the "quality" of democracy. Within these discursive labyrinths, critical thinking has been lost, trapped within the prevailing logic of liberal democratisation without questioning its foundations and limitations.

VIII

Latin America has produced many surprises despite the violent and massive counterinsurgency policies of military and civilian governments, the orthodox application of neoliberal policies that tore the social fabric, intimidated labour, and promoted individualism, and the strident discourse on democratisation and the multiple elections. Over a brief period, the political scene in Latin America has reconstructed once destroyed social movements, with an ongoing capacity to resist and generate projects, including the formation of new political parties that later form governments. In diverse corners, towns, and cities of the region, collective responses are emerging to the projects of the dominant sectors and of the so-called popular governments.

Beginning in the 1990s, the "old mole" of history re-emerged in the region in the form of diverse organisational structures at different moments in time. Miners, peasants, indigenous peoples, students, workers, the urban poor, the underemployed and the unemployed are the main agents in this new phase. They have adopted various forms of struggle and confront the powers that be at various levels. The most relevant crystallisation of this diversified process was the creation and first years of mobilisation of the Ejército Zapatista de Liberación Nacional (EZLN) in Mexico, the Landless Workers' Movement (MST) in Brazil and the eruption of significant indigenous movements. Other similar occurrences include the massive popular uprising that ousted Fernando de la Rua's government in

Argentina, indigenous mobilisations in Bolivia and Ecuador that rose up in defence of water and land rights and that overthrew various neoliberal governments, the popular resistance in Venezuela and Honduras in response to counterinsurgent coups, the Oaxaca Commune that emerged in Mexico in 2006-2007 initially as a mass popular response to the repression of the teachers' movement, the popular governments that took office in Bolivia and Venezuela, and the massive and long-lasting student protests in Chile for free, quality public education.

IX

Strategic Challenges

The triumph of the Cuban Revolution brought a series of old and new problems to the debate, among them, the issue of the revolutionary ruptures in nation-states that remain inscribed within a worldwide capitalist system. How was this situation possible? How can one explain that these revolutions were constructed in the periphery of the system? Could a revolution survive when limited to the borders of nation-states? Was it possible to construct socialism within those borders?

When faced with the first problem, one must note that capital suffers a constituent contradiction: it demands a planetary space as territory for its operations. Nonetheless, its reproduction also requires a national space as one of the bases for the inter-capital competition that characterizes capitalism. This contradiction is the basis of the debates about the possibilities for the survival of revolutions and the construction of socialism. The historical experience appears to confirm that national borders are too narrow, not only for a revolution's survival, but also for building socialism.

Lenin was preoccupied with offering answers to the current problems of the proletarian revolution, and to why these would have more saliency in the periphery of the capitalist system than in its centre, as was evident from the classic writings of Marxism. The Leninist preoccupation in such sense had in the first place a specific theoretical and political objective: to give meaning to the idea of revolution in the peripheral tsarist Russia. Lenin's work draws our attention to the fact that developments in the peripheral zones were influenced by the beginning of capitalism's imperialist phase during the final decades of the 19th century. This phase was characterized by the aggressive dispute between diverse national capitals and their embodiments in the states and financial capital as the greatest and most defined articulation of the world under the logic of capital. Capitalism's imperialist phase also involved the pillaging of the peripheral regions and increased brutality (particularly in these regions), which would prevail over capitalism's civilising dimensions. Lenin indicated that the imperialist chain would tend to break at the weak links, which were to be found in the system's periphery. This is where the system's contradictions, which are interwoven and fused with the local contradictions of capital, would be concentrated. Russia at the beginning of the 20th century was such a case, as this was also true for the other territorial spaces of the system wherein revolution would continue into the 20th century. It is significant that the anti-capitalist revolutions were produced in the peripheral world: Russia, China, Cuba, and Viet Nam.

Faced with the delayed and unfinished development of bourgeois democracy in the periphery, Lenin believed the democratic revolution was a matter of the socialist revolution under proletarian command. The background to Lenin's proposal was an assumption that remains relevant to the explanation that follows in this essay: in the peripheral world, the bourgeoisie is not in a position to carry out the tasks of democratisation. This is not because it lacks the maturity to do so, but flows instead from the dynamics of the reproduction of capital and because its subordination to imperialist capital does not allow it.

X

The Cuban Revolution updated the old Leninist theories while highlighting the current dynamics of revolution in an imperialist phase: the condition of the weakest link of the periphery, the need to incorporate democratic-bourgeois reforms as part of the socialist revolution, along with the problems of the revolution's survival and the limitations of socialist construction when reduced to nation-states. However, the Leninist proposal does not offer an answer to the particularities of how capital is reproduced in the peripheral regions and to the processes by which the contradictions of the capitalist system become synthesized and condensed. The debate about the Cuban Revolution's viability brought to the region, without much mediation, old questions about the character of the Latin American socioeconomic formation and its dynamics. Leftist political forces, organic intellectuals, and progressive professors were some of the main actors in the debate on the issue, which is now referred to as the Cuban process. What were the particularities of that social formation that fuelled revolutions on the continent and throughout the Caribbean islands? It was not just any revolution, but rather one that declared itself to be socialist and demanded that the strategists and social evolutionists set their clocks forward, or change them altogether.

Even before the Cuban Revolution, the debate about the character of Latin America had become polarised between two proposals. The first, which was particularly supported by theorists of the Communist parties, maintained that Latin America—although very advanced in the 20th century—was still a region in which feudal, or rather pre-capitalist, organisation prevailed. They centred their analysis on the dominant social relationships in plantations and other productive agrarian units, and it was these social relationships that defined the character of the social formation. The orthodox Communist Parties' position was first answered by intellectuals of Trotskyist orientation, such as the Argentine historians Luis Vitale and the Chilean Marcelo Segal, who questioned the feudal or pre-capitalist character of the region based on its colonial relationship oriented to capitalist profit. Other important historians supported this stance, such as Sergio Bagú, who pointed out that "the Hispanic-Portuguese colonies of America did not come to life to repeat the feudal cycle, but rather to integrate themselves into the new capitalist cycle that was being inaugurated throughout the world" (1992: 90). For Bagú, "the domination of America is the most important episode in the construction of the world's capitalist system. It turned out to be the most dynamic agent in the accumulation of capital since the beginning of the 16th century, the sine qua non of the historic gestation of the world's capitalist system" (Bagú, 1992: 271-272).

Although the previous reasoning is impeccable, it suffers from a serious deficiency: if this were Latin America's *colonial* role in the gestation of the world's capitalist system, it did not imply the emergence of a process of local reproduction of capital, but rather a simple extension and derivation of the process imposed by the colonising empire. Therefore, it was inappropriate to derive from that reasoning that Latin America *had been capitalist since the 16th century*. One could only speak of a region that is properly capitalist after the transitions toward independence and a process that would bring about the constitution of a local practice of capital reproduction—in the case of the region's integration into the world's capitalist market—and in which various slave-master and pre-capitalist relationships would be integrated.

For the orthodox thinkers and their antagonists in these disputes, the character of the region's revolution was at play: if it was pre-capitalist or feudal, the future revolution should be bourgeois, and only after exhausting this stage could one propose the subject of proletarian revolution. To define the region as capitalist implied, on the contrary, that a proletarian revolution was to be organised.

XI

Although fuelled by different reasons, the old lines of inquiry about the character of Latin America were related to questions formulated by other institutions and scholars who ultimately questioned the universality of the goal of development formulated as occurring in ascending stages with tasks appropriate to each stage (e.g., Rostow, 1961). The "stages of modernization" paradigm in effect highlighted the contrary: that underdevelopment was the flipside of the coin—and a necessary one at that—of development and that only within their mutual relationship could each one explain the other. At the time, formulating these ideas was not an easy task given the weight that academia placed on theories regulated by the assumptions of methodological individualism (in this case, nations replaced individuals). For them, relationships do not exist in the strict sense of the term, but rather only in the exchange of merchandise that takes place in the market. For academia, it was unacceptable to believe that the distinction between who is developed and who is underdeveloped is defined in the heart of these relationships.

Increased attention to development as a problem for the international community—an issue particularly driven by the United States, as the head of the world capitalist system after the end of World War II—led the Economic and Social Council of the United Nations to establish a Special Commission on August 11, 1947 to consider the creation of an Economic Commission for Latin America and the Caribbean (ECLAC).

The presence of the revolution in Cuba and the failures of industrialization in relation to the problems of development and well-being strengthened concerns emerging from a new Marxism.

XIII

What, then, was the nature of Latin American capitalism?

One of the central tasks of the new Latin American Marxism that emerged after the revolutionary process in Cuba was to account for the characteristics of the reproduction of capital at the local level within the context of the world economy. The Cuban Revolution forced a revision of theory on the part of Communist parties, which become increasingly open to the hypotheses of the Marxist dependency theory. A good example is *El desarrollo del capitalismo en America Latina* ("The Development of Capitalism in Latin America"), a book by Ecuadorian communist intellectual Agustín Cueva (1977), who shifted from a steadfastly anti-dependency stance. In it, feudalism is regarded as significant in the region only until the last quarter of the 19th century. Cueva points out that in the strictest sense, the transition from feudalism to capitalism in Latin America did not take place in the 20th century, because "this process, in the most general terms, had already taken place in the oligarchical phase" (Cueva, 1977: 148). He had no qualms about talking about "super-exploitation," the central category of Marini's (2022) proposal, or about the "oligarchical-dependent" means of accumulation.

XIV

The Dialectics of Dependency

Due to their pertinence to the social sciences in general, we note two epistemological contributions of Ruy Mauro Marini's (2022) *The Dialectics of Dependency*:

1. It uses a holistic perspective to account for the characteristics of capital reproduction in a dependent economy. Since it is integrally connected to the movements and processes of the capitalist world economy, Marini had to break with a focus on partial aspects, in this case within the economy. Instead, he analysed the whole process of reproduction, which integrates circulation and production in the local and international spheres. Marini looked for an explanation of the whole, the underlying active unity in the fragments presented by the phenomenal (Osorio, 2012).

2. It represents the unity between the economic and political spheres. Since the disciplines in academia are fragmented, *The Dialectics of Dependency* is an analysis that pertains to the economy. However, it is also a political analysis. Its formulation of the characteristics of the reproduction of capital in dependent capitalism, sustained by super-exploitation, immediately reveals the conditions that determine the possible modes for the creation of community life and the relationships between different social classes that, at the core of that reproduction, take shape by means of contradictions and conflicts.

This holistic perspective, which emphasizes the unity of the economy and politics, makes clear that the tensions leading to rupture and the revolutionary processes present in the region cannot be explained by isolated or fragmented processes and social formations. Rather, such an analysis requires us to examine the tendencies occurring throughout the region, which took form in particular social times and spaces.

XVI

Why have debates about the character of Latin America been set aside, if not completely erased from current discussions? Diagnoses by international or academic organizations, whether of the entire region or the sub-regions of specific economies, flow from implicit assumptions about the regional character. These assumptions are present in the categories used or remain hidden in the background and must be unveiled.

Assumptions concerning the Latin American region are inscribed in stages leading to development. They are present, with more or less force, when one speaks of "economies in development", "patterns of development", "backward economies", "developing economies", "immature economies", etc. In each case, the image is one of moving toward the goal of development (becoming developed).7 To do this, one must remove obstacles, promote forces, and/or resume correct routes. Also operative is the idea of a lack of maturity. Maturation is possible with a few readjustments and changes that would allow greater acceleration.

These formulations and their assumptions have gained tremendous force in international organizations and in academia. They are not even debated in academia, where such debate would be both appropriate and pertinent. Debate is absent because the issue was suppressed instead of being resolved; the previously unstated and implicit ideas were assumed to be the relevant ones. If a critical observation is formulated, one is immediately shown an example of spectacular growth in Southeast Asia during recent decades to settle the discussion. However, if development and underdevelopment are opposite sides of the coin, one should inquire about the degree of dependence and backwardness generated in some other

---

7   To speak of developed and underdeveloped is no small matter. They are terms that "radically altered the way the world was seen. Until then, North/South relations had been organized largely in accordance with the colonizer/colonized opposition. The new 'developed/underdeveloped' dichotomy proposed a different relationship.... Every state was equal de jure, even if it was not (yet) de facto. Colonized and the colonizer had belonged to two different and opposed universes.... Now, however, 'underdeveloped' and 'developed' were members of a single family" (Rist 2009,73—74).

regions of the world that made South Korea's current prosperity possible. From the 1950s onward, the United States and Japan provided crucial support for South Korea's economy in the form of large loans and aid during the tense Cold War years. Such financial contributions meant greater dependence and backwardness in other economies and regions. These resources came from capitalist profits appropriated from other regions, not from the pockets of US or Japanese taxpayers, or from the profits of local or transnational businesses.8 It is also true that beyond such "help," the current achievements were made possible by a strong state and the political discipline imposed upon the entire society, including businesspeople.

Assumptions about universal stages of development are also present in the undying faith some exhibit in technological and scientific innovation. For them, resolving the problem of Latin American underdevelopment lies in investing a larger portion of GDP in science and technology. Thus, what was originally a source of the problem becomes its solution. If the solution is so readily available to the region's political class and businesspeople, why have steps in that direction not been taken? It could not be because they are uneducated (even if some of them indeed are).

Why, after two centuries of independence, have the dominant sectors not resolved something that appears to be so simple? Perhaps it is not a lack of will, but rather structural processes that make such economic and political efforts ineffective, since those technological and scientific advances can now be acquired on the world market or form part of the investment packages of foreign capital in the region. Generating the conditions to create centres for technological and scientific innovation requires significant amounts of capital that must be deducted from immediate accumulation, profit, and luxury consumption. Also needed is a strong state capable of coalescing the forces motivated to do so and discipline on the level of South Korea. In Latin America, where are the willing and disciplined businesspeople needed for that effort? Where is the political class? Why even undertake this effort if technological and scientific innovation

---

8   See Giacomán (1988).

can be acquired abroad while relying on super-exploitation to generate profits?

The scientific and technological development the region needs to overcome dependence is not a budgetary matter. Instead, it is a political issue involving the creation of a new state, new social relationships, and the emergence of new subjects capable of the task. The logic of dominant capital in the dependent world impedes such developments. Despite this, there are those who claim that it is possible to become a "knowledge society." Any isolated example of innovation in the region is projected as a paradigm of anticipated development. Scholars and policymakers then produce weighty tomes that repeat the advantages and qualities of the great development models, without the slightest bit of critical analysis. After all, the diagnosis is that we are not developed because we have yet to do that which the developed have done, particularly in terms of research and technological innovation.

Although capitalism has been around for at least five centuries and the Industrial Revolution took place two and one-half centuries ago, a historical case cannot be easily made that confirms a theory of development that proposes that any economy, without direct or indirect links to others for the appropriation of value, has attained "development" due to its solitary internal effort. However, the contrary can be confirmed: "developed countries" have reached that status by relying on a substantial contribution from the colonies and/or economies and regions that they have plundered, or from the creation of mechanisms that allow for the reappropriation of what had previously been expropriated by others. The power of this discourse, however, does not rest on its ability to prove its claims, but rather on its ability to impose truths.

Discussions of underdevelopment and dependence have not been set aside because new theories have emerged that better explain the Latin American reality. Rather, the problem is related to the full-blown counterrevolutionary process active in Latin America since the 1960s and 1970s. That process is evident in other shapes and forms in the developed world's policies, from dominant neoliberalism to the Washington Consensus. This has affected academia generally and the region's academy in particular;

moreover, the failure of socialism is not unrelated. It became commonplace for certain forms of critical thought to oppose the atrocities carried out by capital in all aspects of social life, all the while using language that does not fundamentally break with the interpretive frameworks that emerged to justify and defend capitalism. This was done without theoretically or conceptually confronting capitalism's processes.

References

Badiou, Alain (2010), *Segundo manifiesto por la filosofía*, Buenos Aires, Manantial.

Bagú, Sergio (1992), *Economía de la sociedad colonial. Ensayo de historia comparada de América Latina*, México, Grijalbo-CONACULTA.

Cueva, Agustín (1977), *El desarrollo del capitalismo en América Latina*, México, Siglo XXI.

Fajnzylber, Fernando (1989), *Industrialización en América Latina: de la "caja negra" al "casillero vacío"*, Santiago, Cuadernos de CEPAL núm. 60.

Feijoo, María Cecilia (2010) "Marx, el jacobinismo negro y la experiencia subalterna de la modernidad. El caso de la revolución antiesclavista de Saint-Domingue", *Herramienta Web*, n. 6.

Giacomán, Ernesto Marcos (1988), "Las exportaciones como factor de arrastre del desarrollo industrial. La experiencia del Sudeste de Asia y sus enseñanzas para México", en *Comercio Exterior*, vol. 38, n. 4, México.

González Callejas, José Luis (2011), *La forma democrática de la disolución estatal mexicana*, México, Departamento de Relaciones Sociales, UAM-Xochimilco.

Grüner, Eduardo (2007) "El 'lado oscuro' de la modernidad. Apuntes (latinoamericanos) para ensayar en clave crítica", *Confines*, número 23, Buenos Aires, Fondo de Cultura Económica, diciembre.

Hobsbawm, Eric (1995), *Age of Extremes: The Short Twentieth Century, 1914-91*, Abacus.

Huntington, Samuel P. (1991), *The Third Wave: Democratization in the Late Twentieth Century*, University of Oklahoma Press.

Marini, Ruy Mauro (2022), *The Dialectics of Dependency*, New York, Monthly Review Press.

Marini, Ruy Mauro (1978), "Las razones del neodesarrollismo", *Revista Mexicana de Sociología*, México, Instituto de Investigaciones Sociales, UNAM.

Marx, Karl (1976), *Capital. Volume 1*, London/New York, Penguin.

Osorio, Jaime (2001), *Violencia y crisis del Estado. Estudios sobre Mexico*, Mexico, UAM-X, Departamento de Relaciones Sociales.

Osorio, Jaime (2012). *Estado, biopoder, exclusión. Análisis desde la lógica del capital*, Barcelona, Anthropos-UAM.

Pérez Soto, Carlos (2008), *Desde Hegel. Para una crítica radical de las ciencias sociales*, México, Itaca.

Rist, Gilbert (2009), *The History of Development: From Western Origins to Global Faith*, Third Edition, New Delhi, Academic Foundation.

Rostow, Walt W. (1990), *The Stages of Economic Growth*, Third Edition, New York, Cambridge University Press.

Sunkel, Osvaldo and Pedro Paz (1970), *El subdesarrollo latinoamericano y la teoría del desarrollo*, México, Siglo XXI.

Valenzuela Feijóo, José (1991), *Aníbal Pinto. América Latina: una visión estructuralista*, México, Facultad de Economía, UNAM.

Zizek, Slavoj (2009a), *First as Tragedy, Then as Farce*, London, Verso.

Zizek, Slavoj (2009b), *Violence*, London. Profile Books Ltd.

Fundamentals of Labour Super-exploitation

Introduction

After its formulation by Ruy Mauro Marini as the defining category of dependent capitalism, the concept of labour super-exploitation has been the subject of sharp discussion and criticism. Theoretical, but also political, reasons are at the basis of these discussions. We will begin by explaining the theory. Critics have raised objections that detract from the sharpest edges of "super-exploitation" as the central concept for understanding dependent capitalism and, at the same time, they blunt its main political consequences.

Exploitation and super-exploitation: and some criticisms

If we understand by exploitation in general the process of a non-producer appropriating other people's labour, in capitalism this process takes the particular form of appropriating the value that exceeds the value of labour-power. In other words, by producing value in the labour process, the worker has the capacity to replace the exchange-value (equivalent to the wage) of their own labour-power, *and* to generate *additional value*, the "surplus-value", which capital appropriates as its property.

Super-exploitation is a *particular form of exploitation*. The particularity is that it is an exploitation in which *the value of labour-power is violated*. This is the special quality of super-exploitation as a form of exploitation. Such violation can be carried out by different mechanisms, either in the market, at the moment of purchase and sale of labour-power, or by "abnormal", extensive or intensive wear and tear in the labour process itself. In all cases, the wage received is no longer equivalent, since it does not cover the full daily value of the labour-power. This is what Marini refers to when he points out that "super-exploitation is defined ... by the greater exploitation of the worker's physical strength ... and tends normally to be

47

expressed in the fact that the *labour-power is remunerated below its real value*" (Marini, 2022: 166; emphasis added).

In several passages of *The Dialectics of Dependency*, Marini speaks of "super-exploitation of labour" or that "labour is remunerated below its value". But reading the book as a whole leaves no doubt that the author refers to the violation of the value of labour-*power*, as he specifies in the post-script of the small book, from where the previous quotation comes. Pages later Marini establishes *the weight and significance of super-exploitation in the reproduction of capital in dependent economies*, when after debating and clarifying some erroneous remarks he indicates: "These are some of the substantive issues raised in my essay [Part I of *The Dialectics of Dependency*] that called for greater detail and for clarification. They reaffirm the central thesis sustained therein, that is, *that the basis of dependency is the super-exploitation of labor*" (Marini, 2022: 166; emphasis added).

Super-exploitation is a central issue of labour exploitation in dependent economies, *it has consequences on the whole process of how capital is reproduced*, and for the subordinate status of these economies in accumulation at the level of the world system. Failure to consider this general vision is one of the main limitations of the criticisms and misunderstandings of the problem, as super-exploitation is considered in an isolated way, so that many criticisms end up becoming entangled in purely formal matters, relegating the set of relations that determine it and that it itself determines. Among the most significant criticisms and confusions about super-exploitation are the following:

- Marx bases exploitation in capitalism on respect for the value of labour-power. Moreover, he sustains the growing weight of the law of value in the dynamics of capitalism. From these premises it is concluded that a theory based on the violation of value cannot have consistency with Marx, nor can it be assumed as Marxist. The positivist bias of Marxism and the ignorance of negation are at the base of these confusions.

- Super-exploitation refers to past forms of exploitation, only pertinent to the initial moments of capitalism, linked to absolute surplus-value. Industrial capitalism aims to sustain itself in the production of relative surplus-value. Therefore "however significant its historical importance" super-exploitation "is of no theoretical interest" (Marini, 2022: 161).

- Wages express the value of labour-power. It is therefore enough to follow wage movements to determine what happens to the value of the latter. These fluctuations in wages (and in the value of labour-power) may be marked by problems of competition (such as oversupply of available hands) or by impositions of force that decree decreases in wages. In all cases, this in turn implies decreases in the value of labour-power. Price and value, in these visions, end up being always the same, which does not explain Marx's efforts to determine value, if it was enough to observe the behaviour of prices.9

- The incorporation of women, adolescents and children into the work process brings with it a depreciation of the value of adult labour-power. This allows the formation of a "family wage" that alters the value of labour-power, which is then "determined, not only by the labour-time necessary to maintain the individual adult worker, but also by that necessary to maintain his family" (Marx, 1976: 518). This brief statement by Marx, written in a chapter whose subject is not the value of labour-power and which in the context of his work can be pointed out as wrong, is assumed as a criterion that would modify the central statements made by the author in other sections where he considers the problem of the value of the labour-power. Its consequences in terms of increased exploitation and super-exploitation are evident. Hence the ease with which these indications are assumed by certain academic sectors, governmental and international organizations.

- Super-exploitation has ceased to constitute a particularity of the exploitation of dependent capitalism, as it has extended to the

---

9   On this position, see Valenzuela Feijóo (1997).

whole of the capitalist world economy: its signs, in the midst of the current world crisis, are evident. The apparent radicality of this approach ends up diluting the particularity of the reproduction of capital in dependent capitalism, which is thereby put into question.10

- Super-exploitation is a compensation mechanism that is triggered in dependent economies by value transfers from dependent economies to central economies. But this mechanism, it is stated rather strangely, should not be confused with ways to increase the rate of surplus-value. But more serious is the indeterminacy of super-exploitation itself, reduced or assimilated to exploitation without further ado, but sharpened, leaving this category in a confused and imprecise theoretical status.11

With these approaches as a backdrop, let us move on to the analysis of some theoretical issues that allow us to highlight the misunderstandings on which these and other points rest.

On the law of value

Value is an abstraction that only has social consistency, since "not an atom of matter enters into the objectivity of commodities as values; in this it is the direct opposite of the coarsely sensuous objectivity of commodities as physical objects" (Marx, 1976: 138). It is a definite social relation that takes form as value in a particular world, capitalism, where the production of commodities has been generalized and work is carried out by independent producers that only validate their individual labour as aliquot parts of the labour of society.

In the first instance value is presented in the *form* of exchange-value, and this in the price *form* and the money *form*. The price form in turn is expressed as a price of production and as a market price. In this process of

---

10   This is argued by Adrian Sotelo (2003; 2012). Carlos Eduardo Martins (2019) takes a similar position.
11   See Marcelo Dias Carcanholo (2013).

unfolding or manifesting, distortions are produced, one of which is the difference between value and price. Prices of production and market prices show that not every capitalist appropriates the value he produces, but a surplus-value that may be above or below that value.12 However, the rise or fall of market prices has a centre of gravity, and that is the market value of commodities.13

The distortion between value and price is only a pale expression of what happens in social life of capitalism. The world that capital builds, in its unfolding of the essence to the diverse phenomenal and apparent forms that it assumes, is an "enchanted world, inverted and put on its head" because, among other reasons, relations between men assume the form of relations between things, which as "autonomous figures endowed with a life of their own" (Marx, 1976: 165), fetishise social relations, obscuring the processes of social life.

Essence, appearance and fetishisation

Appearance is the essence itself in the determination of Being, says Hegel (2010: 418-9), so the question that must accompany any reflection on social relations in capitalism is why they take certain forms *that are hidden by their very form of appearance.*

The essence of capital, as well as of value and of the State, for example, is not expressed in an open and transparent way. They do so under *forms* in which an opaque and distorted appearance emerges, that is, under *fetishised* forms.14 In capitalism all this makes sense because capital builds a social world sustained in the *real fiction* of free and equal human beings. This does not mean ignoring the fact that the rupture of the relations of subjection and vassalage of the serfs establishes the basis for the "freedom"

---

12 The price of production is the commodity's cost plus the average rate of profit. These matters are explained by Marx in *Capital. Volume 3* (1981).

13 "Market value ... forms in turn the centre around which market prices fluctuate" (Marx, 1981: 279).

14 Marx points out: "all science would be superfluous if the form of appearance of things directly coincided with their essence" (1981: 956).

of the proletariat. However, that freedom, like going to the market to sell one's labour, will be marked by the original coercion or violence of the dispossession of means of production. At the same time, by capital appropriating the surplus-value that the worker produces, he reproduces from one day to another his lack of means of life and production, so that the coercion and despotism of capital continue to operate, making felt their daily presence in the market. Therefore, in real terms, "the worker belongs to capital before he has sold himself to the capitalist" (Marx, 1976: 723) and he "must incessantly be re-incorporated into capital as its means of valorization, which cannot get free of capital, and whose enslavement to capital is only concealed by the variety of individual capitalists to whom it sells itself" (Marx, 1976: 764; emphasis added). The apparent freedom of the worker thus presents as the negation of very essence: slavery and subjection to the despotism of capital.

If the social relations of exploitation and domination were simply expressed, that fiction of freedom would break like soap bubbles. Social relations then demand particular forms of manifesting themselves and becoming in the world that reinforce that imaginary. At the same time it is necessary that they reach consistency and reality (hence *real fiction*). There are examples: such as market relations of things (money) for things (products); prices (that rise and fall by supply and demand) and not value; the State as an arbiter, or as social contract, and not as condensed class violence; profit, as expression of increased wealth resulting from all capital, and not surplus-value, new value generated by variable capital; the wage as payment for labour and not for labour-power; electoral citizenship as political equality (each head only counts as one vote), in a world where economic and political inequality reigns.

General analysis of capital

Marx maintains that the more capitalist market relations develop, the greater the consistency of the law of value, thus constituting a gravitational centre in the determination and fluctuations of prices. However, Marx himself points out many times in his work the diverse procedures that make it both possible and necessary for capital to violate this tendential law. I emphasize one by way of example: when Marx refers to the mechanisms that counteract the falling rate of profit, he indicates as a second resource the "reduction of wages below their value", and in the footnote he adds "that is, *below the value of labour power*". In the short seven-line text accompanying this procedure it is stated: "We simply make an empirical reference to the point here, since .... it has nothing to do with the general analysis of capital". Marx ends with "It is *nonetheless one of the most important factors in stemming the tendency of the rate of profit to fall*" (Marx, 1981: 342; emphases added). This last affirmation seems to contradict the indication of the growing validity of value as an element that defines exchanges. It should be noted that "contradictions" of this type are present in the treatment of all the problems addressed.

The first answer to this way of reasoning that Marx formulates in the quotation: for the "general analysis of capital", is that for the level of abstraction of his reflection in *Capital*, it is unnecessary to introduce modifications to the assumptions made, because that analysis requires that "The transformation of money into capital has to be developed on the basis of the immanent laws of the exchange of commodities, in such a way that *the starting-point is the exchange of equivalents*"(Marx, 1976: 268-9; emphasis added). That is why he insists that "pushing the wage of the worker below the value of his labour-power" is "despite the important part which this method plays in practice", excluded from his considerations, "by our assumption that *all commodities, including labour power, are bought and sold at their full value*" (Marx, 1976: 431; emphasis added).

The assumptions in *Capital* and their objectives

To unlock the limits faced by classical political economy on the value/labour problem from the point at which it arrived: it is labour that generates value, implicit in the idea of the "general analysis of capital" (at a high level of abstraction), no matter how much historical/concrete capital behaved in a manner exceeding those assumptions (with greater concreteness).

This approach implied separating simple elements in order to make them more complex in their development. Using this method Marx manages to break with the wall raised by the classic political economy, he shows that labour, in capitalism, has a double dimension: it is concrete labour that produces use-values, and it is simultaneously abstract labour, the generator of value, in historical conditions where labour-power itself becomes a commodity, and that when at work has the particular quality of producing more value than it is worth, leaving manifest the origin of surplus-value and wealth *in capitalism. To explain all this, it was not necessary to introduce more concrete problems, such as operative violations of value.*

But Marx's critique of classical political economy wants to go further. It needs to show the historicity of capitalism, first in the sense that its categories are only appropriate for the capitalist organization of social life, and not for all modes of production; and second, that capitalist production is also a historical production, so it must realise the processes that it generates itself and that point to its end. It is from here that Marx's theoretical arguments stand out, showing the tendencies of capitalism to crises, and within this argumentation, to the mechanisms to counteract such tendencies.

In this second effort Marx again limits himself to certain assumptions (such as that prices are equal to value, a matter that he will modify in later chapters, where value will emerge as prices of production and market prices), those necessary in terms of the abstraction/concretion process he carries out,15 to highlight the negativity that causes that "the true barrier to capitalist production is *capital itself*" (Marx, 1981:358). From these assumptions we analyze the processes that tend to favour the fall of the rate of profit, which precipitates the crises, and the mechanisms to counteract that fall (although they never succeed in suppressing the tendency). But

---

15   It is important to emphasize that in spite of sustaining certain assumptions, others are being concretized inasmuch as they allow Marx to advance into those problems that he wants to emphasise to understand capitalism. In this sense surplus-value is concretised as profit, for example, and with it opens the door to explaining the tendency of the rate of profit to fall, and the way towards crises.

the general tendencies of the falling rate of profit and crises, and the mechanisms to counteract them, are accentuated at levels of greater concretion where the law of value is violated. This occurs, for example, when certain capitals can establish commodity prices that are significantly above their values and prices of production, due to the monopolisation reached by its high technological sophistication, thereby appropriating value through unequal exchanges with economies that produce primary goods with minor technological complexities. Or, when faced with a falling rate of profit, capital pays wages below the value of labour-power to counteract that fall, which we have seen that Marx points out, but does not analyse, "because it has nothing to do with the general analysis of capital" (Marx, 1981: 342).

Problems such as those mentioned above, which no longer fall under the "general analysis of capital", but under more concrete modalities of capitalism deployment, must necessarily consider processes that violate the assumptions that that analysis required. The historicity present in those assumptions thus reaches greater concreteness.

Logic, negation, levels of abstraction, universal/particular[16]

For the purposes of this exposition, let us separate the theoretical-philosophical elements imbricated in the previous considerations. One is logical. For formal logic if it is said that this-is, it cannot be affirmed simultaneously, without entering into a logical conflict, that this-is not, since it infringes against the principles of identity and non-contradiction of formal logic. But "to understand or describe the complexity of what is real" and of being, as Pérez Soto rightly points out, formal logic is too poor.[17] For a task of this magnitude, another logic is required, a logic that is ontological and

---

16   Throughout this section I rely freely on Pérez Soto (2008)

17   Carlos Pérez Soto, "Lógica ontológica y lógica formal", in http://grupohegel.blogspot.co
      m/2010/01/logica-ontologica-y-logica-formal.html. For Herbert Marcuse (1955: 131)
      "formal logic accepts the world- form as it is and gives some general rules for theoretical
      orientation to it. Dialectical logic on the other hand, rejects any claim of sanctity for the
      given, and shatters the complacency of those living under its rubric".

dialectic, that assumes negativity and with it contradiction as its own. Marx's theory is a theory of being and its negation, it is necessary to emphasise the second aspect. By thinking of the Being as simultaneous non-Being, the dialectic assumes negativity in the Being,18 the inner struggle that makes it possible to think of the Being as a "going on", a Being "with internal tension that constantly becomes the other of itself" (Pérez Soto 2008: 162). In short, a becoming, that is contradictory.

If the processes are simultaneously their own negation,19 it is possible to understand that the civilization that derives from capitalism is simultaneously barbaric;20 that development has underdevelopment inscribed in its bosom; that the same processes that generate wealth are those that generate poverty. With this we manage to break with the dichotomies,21 so claimed by the dominant knowledge, and instead of thinking of "things", isolated and still (as each element of the dichotomy), we can think of relationships, and in the way those relationships are projected in the fetishised world as reified "things". Instead of asking ourselves about the social relations that constitute value, and the forms that conceal it, exchange value, money, prices, profit, etc., we tend to take the forms as "things", but also without the negativity that constitutes them. So value becomes something given, still, fixed, without conflicts, or at most a simple conflict and

---

18   "Being is non-being in essence. Its nullity in itself constitutes the negative nature of the essence itself" (Hegel, 2010: 348). "Negativity is the essential tension, that which is properly the essence, the pure relationship, from which the Being turns out to be. It is the constituent activity as such. It is, in a way, the most basic concept that can be attributed to the activity of Being. (…). The negativity acts positing the Being, but also dissolving it."

19   Processes that have negation inscribed, but not as "opposition", that is, "conflict in the usual sense of struggle between two entities that already exist in a previous way by themselves", but that only are and are constituted in the relationship.

20   The angel of Walter Benjamin's story is a good plastic image of the above. He walks towards progress, but his head turns to look at the destruction he is leaving behind. Various images can be searched on the internet, although Benjamin had as a reference a painting by Paul Klee in his thesis.

21   Dichotomies are present in the most varied fields of analysis and always force us to choose "this or that". Thus we have: determination or contingency; democracy or authoritarianism; nomothetic sciences or idiographic sciences; subject or object; State or market; public or private; included or excluded, with a long etcetera. The relationship never appears that simultaneously incorporates both extremes.

negation between use-value and value. As a social relation value contains its own negation, as the breaking or the violation of value. *The violation of value* is none but the *other side of the display of value*, in a world in which an unbridled desire is unleashed by surplus labour, by living labour, the only source of value. *Attacking and violating the value of labour-power then emerges as the necessary counterpart to the expansion and development of value.*

The questions that remain to be solved are why this negativity ends up taking form as the basis for the reproduction of capital in some regions and spaces of the capitalist world system (such as dependent economies), and why this negation is still latent and present even in the regions and economies that seem to have banished it (the central economies). The Marxist dependency theory, in the hands of Marini, formulated answers to these questions.

The lack of understanding that Marxist reflection develops under logical and philosophical procedures different from prevailing knowledge systems, leads to unilateral judgments about a Marx fascinated by technology and productive forces, insensitive to the problems that capital generates in nature, a thinker inscribed in modernity, when all his reflection and his way of reflecting is a critique of that modernity, of capital, and its knowledge. Also when it is affirmed that Marx is a eurocentric thinker of progress, leaving aside the general *corpus* of a work that is the most radical critique of capitalism and its progress,[22] in the framework of the conversion of the development of the productive forces in a process of reversion against the workers and nature.

The third question that we wish to highlight from Marx's reflection refers to the levels of analysis (abstraction and concretion) inscribed in the *corpus* of Marxist theory. To decipher the problems in which classical political economy was trapped and to emphasise the historical character of capitalism Marx abstracts simple elements, which implies leaving aside

---

22   A question forgotten by some currents and authors of the so-called "postcolonial studies".

others (such as the violation of value), to establish from there the bridges to more concrete analyses, that is to say with more elements and greater determinations. In those more concrete analyses the demands and limitations raised in the previous levels of greater abstraction are not sustained. With this we could not advance in concretion, as new determinations, new elements and processes make a *more concrete* history, a history that deepens in its condition of "synthesis of multiple determinations".

Universal capitalism, finally, in its *historical* unfolding, claims to be thought of the effective reality of the *particulars* that have taken shape in its unfolding, such as the conformation of capitalism as a *world system* with diverse capitalisms *operating in a differentiated manner in world accumulation*; that is the central or imperialist economies, and peripheral or dependent economies. Capitalism is thus constituted in a *differentiated universality* which demands *new concepts and categories* to be learned, to comprehend the integrated processes and relations that redefine the universal, and because *particularities generate real diversity*, effecting the novelty of difference, making capitalism the *unity of the diverse*.23

From what has been said we can understand the fallacious orthodoxy of those who maintain that if any new term is not found in *Capital*, for that simple reason it would be wrong. This has been another aspect of criticism to the notion of super-exploitation and in general to the Marxist dependency theory. In other words, particulars, because of their differentiated relationship in the accumulation of capital worldwide, *generate in turn particular internal forms of the reproduction of capital*. To account for the originality of that reproduction in dependent capitalism, in its imbrication with central capitalism, is the task that Marini tries to solve in *The Dialectics of Dependency*. The theory developed in *The Dialectics of Dependency* is perhaps the most ambitious and finished formulation of the *particularity* of dependent capitalism. For Marini, the assumptions prevailing in *Capital* cannot be taken for granted, since the analysis seeks to explain a more concrete and specific capitalism, a form of the negativity in the development

---

23   Here I lean freely on Pérez Soto (2008), chapter IX.

of capitalism, where *super-exploitation is now the articulating and defining notion of this form of capitalist reproduction.*

On the Value of Labour Power

There are many particularities of the commodity labour-power in relation to its value, and the redefinitions it suffers at various levels of analysis, which makes it difficult to approach its determination. We will highlight, however, some relevant elements, to begin to delve into the problem and in particular into the issues that raise more discussion.

a) The value of the necessary means of subsistence, which allow the producer to obtain a rest and replenish their energies, returning to work under the same "conditions as regards health and strength". This includes the goods that cover the so-called *essential needs*, which have a *historical and moral* determination. This refers to the particular way in which in different times and societies workers feed, dress, rest, etc., and depend on the "level of civilization" and "the conditions in which, and consequently on the habits and expectations with which, the class of free workers has been formed" (Marx, 1976: 275).

This implies that the mass or volume of products that make up a basket of wage goods cannot be decided without considering those historical and cultural conditions, including for example products because of their low price or for criteria of "what should be" a good diet. On the other hand, it must be considered that the productive development of a society involves converting certain luxury products into wage goods, which are integrated to the necessary means of life of the working population. At the beginning of the 21st century televisions, refrigerators or common cell phones would fall in this category. They form part of the sociability and common life that capital has established. In this way *the value of labour-power is in tension* from the double process that increases the mass of essential products, which leads to an increase of its value, and the increase of productivity, particularly in the production of wage goods, which leads to them becoming cheaper.

b) The value of labour-power has a double dimension, its daily value and its total value. And the *daily value* is determined by its *total value*. Marx refers to this when he indicates that "the value of one day's labour-power is estimated ... on the basis of its average normal average duration, or the normal duration of the life of a worker and on the basis of the appropriate normal standard of conversion of living substances into motion as it applies to the nature of man" (Marx, 1976: 664). The same idea is reiterated a few pages later: "We know that the daily value of labour-power is calculated upon a certain duration of the worker's life" (Marx, 1976: 679). This implies that the producer must present themselves to the labour market a certain number of years, guided by their health conditions and the life expectancy reached in specific historical periods, where their *working life* must constitute a part of their *total life*, to a limit that is defined by the contending wills of the capitalists and the workers, in "a prolonged and more or less concealed civil war between the capitalist class and the working class" (Marx, 1976: 412), just like the battles over the length of the working day (Marx, 1976:282). Here the class struggle is established in the dispute for the duration of the day, and *therefore for the price of labour-power*, to determine that it does not move away from the value.

The wear and tear on labour-power in those years of working life, whether by extension or intensity, must be developed under "normal" conditions. When the working day is prolonged, the wear and tear on labour-power increases, thus increasing its value, i.e., what is required to replenish it. The payment of overtime can be a way of expressing this increase in the wage. But it may be that even the wage increase does not compensate fully for the extra wear and tear from longer hours of work, so that even if more the extra wage will fall below the value of labour-power. Such greater wear and tear can shorten the worker's useful life, that is to say, it violates the total value of the labour-power, even though the higher daily wage could give the idea that it rises above that value. At root, capital receives the labour of several working days and pays the wages of one working day. The worker complains "You pay me for one day's labour-power, while you use three days of it" and points out that "Using my labour and despoiling it are quite different things" (Marx, 1976:343). In this case the worker's voice is highlighted by Marx, resisting capital as it appropriates the workers' *life fund*. However, there is a point at which no wage increase will end up compensating for the wear and tear of the work force by the extension of the workday, because "beyond this point deterioration increases in geometrical progression, and all the requirements for the normal reproduction and functioning of labour-power cease to be fulfilled" (Marx, 1976: 664).

With increases in productivity capital can produce more with the same or with less wear and tear on the work force. If that productivity increase is in sectors that produce wage goods, it allows the reduction of the value of those goods and this can be expressed in a reduction of the value of the labour-power. If wages do not fall, they will tend to be above the reduced value of labour-power. If they do fall in proportion to the reduction in the prices of wage goods, the reduced value of labour-power and wages will tend to coincide.

The intensification of work implies an "increased expenditure of labour in a given time" (Marx, 1976: 660) so that although the number of products or use-values increases, the value and price of each one does not decrease. As in the case of the extension of the working day, with the increase in intensity the increase in daily wages (and therefore the idea that wages can end up above the value of labour-power) can be accompanied by a violation of the total value of the labour-power, by reducing the useful life of the worker.

c) The value of labour-power includes the reproduction of new labourers, so it includes the *reproduction of the family of the workers*, and especially of their children. The definition of the working age is a historical and cultural product, but in no case can it contemplate the incorporation of children into work processes, nor of adolescents, whose physical and spiritual capacities are developing, and the work threatens their living conditions, whether by the effort required (carrying bulks or other objects of weight for adults), and by taking time away from rest and recreation, which are vital for their development and for their education. The idea of a "family wage", made up of the work of various family members (if not all), including adolescents and children, has been assumed without much criticism. By this procedure capital would be able to lower the value of the labour-power of adults and with the sum of wages of adults, adolescents and children, cover the needs of a family. Despite some formulations of Marx in this sense,24 I consider that the general spirit of his work is that the central factors determining the value of labour-power depend on whoever sells it must be the *"free proprietor* of his own labour-capacity, hence of his person" (Marx, 1976: 271). Here we would have adults throwing onto the labour market children or adolescents who do not have the capacity to make decisions and to assume responsibilities on what and how to work, nor for how much to work.

The fact that adult labourers have to take on additional incomes from their children in order to reproduce themselves and reproduce their families implies a formula that does not correspond to the logic prevailing in the determination of value. It is closer to relations of vassalage or slavery (in the parent-child relationship). This can actually operate, that is not under discussion, but it *cannot be assumed* as a procedure to *define the value of labour-power*. On the contrary, it is more a form of a grotesque *violation of the value of labour-power* committed by adult parents, and which *devastates* in its brutality *the lives of children and adolescents*. In short, the price of labour-power can be driven to subhuman extremes by mechanisms such as those described. But this only indicates the *distance that price can deviate from value*, that is, to what degree super-exploitation can reach. Capital can also subject slave labour to its despotic domination. But no one takes for granted that the value of the labour-power would be calculated on that premise. This type of situation only highlights the barbarism that accompanies the deployment of capital.

Buying and selling labour-power below its value

The grossest and least hidden way to violate the value of labour-power is that in the very process of its purchase-sale capital pays a wage below that

---

24   Which I have described as wrong in the general context of his work. See Marx (1976: 517-519).

value. This process, which breaks with the level of abstraction in which Marx has moved, has such a significance that it is necessary to raise it with force and eloquence: "In the chapters on the production of surplus-value, we constantly assumed that wages were at least, *the value of labour-power*. But *the forcible reduction of the wage of labour beneath its value* plays too important a role in the practical move of affairs for us not to stay with this phenomenon for a moment. In fact, it transforms the *worker's necessary fund for consumption*, within certain limits, *into a fund for the accumulation of capital*" (Marx, 1976: 747-748; emphases added).

After quoting a paragraph by John Stuart Mill in which he affirms that "wages do not contribute, along with labour, to the production of commodities", and where he states in conclusion: "If labour could be had without purchase, wages might be dispensed with", Marx comments that "if the workers could live on air, it would not be possible to buy them at any price". He adds a couple of lines later: "The *constant tendency of capital* is to force the cost of labour back towards *this absolute zero*" (Marx, 1976: 748; emphases added).

Here we can appreciate the real significance of super-exploitation in Marx's perception. He is the first to be aware that the value relationship necessarily has as its other face the tendency to be violated. The fact that he did not approach it theoretically was not because of its irrelevance, as is evident in the previous paragraphs, and in others, but because it implied introducing a problem that removed him from his central concerns in *Capital*.

Marx calls it "redoubled exploitation", at least on three occasions (Marx,1976: 747, 754 and 775).25 "Redoubled exploitation" is a category that I have preferred to use lately, although not here, in order not to introduce unnecessary discussions to the problems addressed concerning "wages below their value". Paolo Santi (1965) uses the notion of "super-

---

25   [Translator's note: this is rendered as "increased exploitation" in the English translations, which has a weaker connotation compared to the Spanish.]

exploitation" I believe for the first time. Marini was familiar with this text, as he refers to it in *The Dialectics of Dependency*.

Super-exploitation and ways to increase the rate of surplus-value

In their praiseworthy interest in highlighting the significance of super-exploitation in dependent capitalism, some authors point out that, as a compensation mechanism arising from the transfer of values to the central world, super-exploitation should be differentiated from the methods used to raise the rate of surplus value, since these are general, inherent to any modality of capitalism, and with that identification super-exploitation would lose its particularity.26

Various problems and confusions are presented here. The first is an indeterminacy concerning super-exploitation. Because even if it is said that it is a compensation mechanism, it must be clarified what that mechanism consists of. Is exploitation increased? There is no way not to promote this increase without resorting to ways to raise the rate of surplus-value, no matter how much one looks for elements to differentiate these from the former. Discarding the idea of the violation of the value of labour-power does not solve the problem. The problem of a super-exploitation thus conceived, which only refers to increasing exploitation, is that *the specificity of exploitation in dependent capitalism is lost*. Where would its particularity lie?

Subject to the forms of exploitation, even if it is said that they are not the same, super-exploitation would be simply a sharpening of those. In short, it would have no particularity whatsoever. If it is assumed that super-exploitation is *a particular form of exploitation*, that in which the value of labour-power is violated, be it daily or in total, the confusion begins to clear up. From this perspective the ways to increase the rate of surplus-value should not be confused, because they do not imply in themselves violating the value of labour-power. The working day can be extended in

---

26   See Carcanholo (2013).

reasonable magnitudes, in limited periods, and the additional payment of overtime could compensate for this greater wear and tear. The same can happen with intensity. Only permanent extensions of the working day cause the life fund to be reduced. All the more so in cases of regular and unreasonable extensions: there is no extra payment to compensate for wear and tear. Only in these cases does this form of increasing the rate of surplus-value become a form of super-exploitation. The same reasoning can be used concerning increased labour intensity.

Only the appropriation of part of the consumption fund or the life fund, to transfer them to the accumulation fund, constitute simultaneously a way of increasing the rate of surplus-value and at the same time forms of super-exploitation. By way of contrast, raising productivity in the branches producing wage goods (without simultaneous increase in intensity) is a way of raising the rate of surplus-value without constituting a form of super-exploitation. We can now reaffirm that super-exploitation is the violation of the value of labour-power and that it is carried out under different forms, where some directly violate the daily value and others, in a mediated way, its total value.

Capitalism and super-exploitation

Super-exploitation was in Marx's reflection an issue that also involved capitalism that we today call central capitalism. His references on the subject are made concerning English capitalism, the most developed form of capitalism of his time. However, as we have already mentioned, he only referred to it in an "empirical" way, without a theoretical treatment. Being a universal process, however, changes occurred from the middle of the 19th century, and in the 20th century, which claim to be necessary to understand in its proper terms the statement of Ruy Mauro Marini that "the foundation of dependency is the super-exploitation of labour" (2022) that gives new meaning to super-exploitation in the functioning of dependent capitalism.

From colonial relations with Latin America, the central economies moved to relations with formally independent nations towards the middle of the 19th century, which are inscribed in a clear international division of labour, some as producers of raw materials and food and buyers of manufactured goods, and others as producers and exporters of industrial goods. This process allows an important shift in the central economies from absolute surplus-value as the predominant form to an economy based on relative surplus-value. The supply of food and raw materials from Latin America to these economies played a fundamental role in this turn, by reducing the prices of wage goods, which made it feasible to reduce necessary labour time, and in turn "free" a wide tranche of labour in the industrial economies from agricultural labour, to engage in manufacturing production. This shift implied the maturation of a form of reproduction in which workers will play an increasingly significant role in the realisation of surplus-value, insofar as they will form a substantial part of the internal market and consumption, without ignoring the role of workers' struggles to shorten the working day in those processes, as well as the demands for better living conditions.

Nor does this mean assuming that the drives of capital to plunder labour in super-exploitative forms were nullified. The real conditions, however, are making it possible for these drives, in their crudest manifestations, to be circumscribed to particular groups of local workers, to the immigrant population and to the sections of the relative overpopulation that manages to get a foothold, albeit temporarily and irregularly, in production. This is as long as the crises are not present, which unleashes the tendencies to violate the extraction and appropriation of value, although this implies reducing to subsistence levels the workers' consumption fund, among some of the main measures.

But this turn also had another important process that had matured. With higher levels of productivity, production of industrial goods and knowledge under monopolistic conditions, the central economies were able to set prices that violated the law of value (and with it the prices of production and market prices of their products), thus managing to appropriate value and labour from the non-industrial economies through unequal exchange. This strengthened the forces towards the elaboration of new and more sophisticated technologies, machines and tools in those economies, as well as increasing the historical and moral components in the value of labour-power, multiplying the civilizing features of capitalism in its relation with the work force in those zones of the capitalist world system. It is imperialist and dependent capital that exploits, not the workers of the central world.

These objective conditions in the reproduction of capital make it possible to understand the greater weight of wages in the imperialist world, and not for reasons such as assuming that the class struggle has been greater or more acute there than in dependent economies. In this kind of reasoning, moreover, the class struggle becomes the master key that explains everything. But what explains the class struggle itself, and the conditions under which it develops? This sociologism does not go very far. This is another reason why Marx wrote *Capital*: to offer an answer that explains the terrain in which the class struggle unfolds in capitalism.

The effects of these processes would move capitalism maturing in Latin American non-industrial economies in the opposite direction. Rather than seeking to compensate value transfers by raising productivity, capital in this part of the world compensated for such value flows by increasing super-exploitation, increasing value production by such means as either through the appropriation of the workers' consumption fund to turn it into a capital accumulation fund, or through the maintenance of long working days. What is important to emphasise is that the dependent form of capitalism took shape with the consumption of the working population constituting a secondary element in relation to the most dynamic sectors, branches or productive units of capital accumulation: in short, a type of capitalism in which workers count more as producers of value than as consumers, so their role in the local market tends to be insignificant. This ties in with the tendency of dependent capitalism to create reproduction patterns turned towards foreign markets. It is a capitalism that is more concerned with the consumer power of workers in the regions where it is exported than those of the local economy. If we analyze the economic history of the Latin American region, we can see that the so-called period of industrialization is only a brief parenthesis in the long history of the predominance of export patterns: the first is the agro-mining exporter, and at present the specialization of production.27

When the process of industrialization began, it seemed that this trend was reversing, and the local bourgeoisie and organizations such as ECLAC played with this imaginary. In reality the illusions were short-lived, the time when the imperialist economies came out of the Second War and the United States began to operate as the new hegemonic economy within the capitalist world system. It was the period in which the local bourgeoisie had exhausted light manufacturing production and had to move on to higher stages, such as the production of consumer durables and capital goods. Instead of channelling their efforts to achieve new stages of production, which demanded a high process of accumulation and raising expenses for the production of science and technology, the already formed local bourgeoisie ended up allying itself with foreign capital, particularly U.S. capital, which, as a result of the application to industry of military technological advances, accelerated the renewal of fixed capital in its economy, which allowed it to put on the market a high mass of machines, equipment and technologies at low cost and with great facilities. In this way, big local capital found a way out to pass to new stages in industrialization, without the economic cost and sacrifice of producing equipment and machinery locally, but it ended up allied with foreign capital, opening the industry to such investments.

Along with putting an end to the nationalist and progressive illusions of the local bourgeoisie, the latter, in alliance with foreign capital, ended up taking up again the same path of reproduction of capital that industrialization was supposed to modify: the generation of a productive structure that tends to move away from the needs of the broad majority of workers. Although in their original economies imported goods and equipment could form part of the production of wage goods (such as durable consumer goods, from refrigerators to automobiles), their production in economies sustained in super-exploitation ends up generating luxury goods,

---

27   On the weight of export patterns in Latin America and the analysis of the new export model see (Osorio, 2012).

destined for small pockets of the population. From what has been said so far we can affirm that *dependency is a particular form of reproduction of capital, sustained by labour super-exploitation,* a form that in turn reproduces the subordination of these economies to the imperialist centres. It is only from *a view on the whole process of reproduction* of capital, and of the *relations* it establishes in that unity, that *super-exploitation reaches its essential significance.* To reflect from this perspective constitutes one of the virtues of Marxism and of the philosophy that constitutes it.

The world system as unity of various forms of capitalism

The capitalist world system constitutes a differentiated unity in a "strong sense": as "the effectiveness of the universal thought as difference" (Pérez Soto, 2008: 166). Unity, because it is the logic of capital, the light "which bathes all the other colours," and "the specific gravity of every being which has materialized within it" (Marx, 1973: 107). It is a general illumination that modifies their particularities. Differentiated, because the negation of the universal constitutes "the effective reality of the particular" and "makes thinkable the real diversity" of the world that capital has built (Pérez Soto, 2008: 165 and 166). Central and imperialist capitalisms and dependent capitalisms constitute some of their forms, inseparable, different in unity and only explainable in the relation that constitutes them.

If there are regions and economies where super-exploitation is the basis for the reproduction of capital, this does not mean that it is not present throughout the capitalist world system. The capitalist civilization has its correlate of barbarism in the very heart of the imperialist countries themselves. The same happens with wealth and its expression in poverty. Or the army of active workers, with underemployed, unemployed and *paupers*. In the same way in dependent capitalism: there are civilizing islets and islets of wealth; there is not only barbarism, poverty, unemployed and underemployed. Not understanding this is what leads authors like Hardt and Negri to point out that these days it makes no sense to distinguish between centres and peripheries. They say that "the sweatshops of New York and Paris can rival those of Hong Kong and Manila." Even stronger is their point that in a world increasingly integrated by the global processes of production, between "the United States and Brazil, Britain and India" there are "no differences of nature, only differences of degree" (Hardt and Negri, 2000: 335). These worlds have been mixed up in a jumble, "the spatial divisions of the three Worlds (First, Second, and Third) have been scrambled so that we continually find the First World in the Third, the Third in the First, and the Second almost nowhere at all" (Hardt and Negri, 2000: XIII). Globalization discourse points to the imaginary that we have reached a stage where all economies find conditions to develop, the more they become global (open their economies, produce for "the world", reduce protectionist barriers, etc.). There is no "unequal exchange," no imperialism, no dependency: curious similarities with the approach of Hardt and Negri, for whom the "Empire" has no geographical settlements; it is the non-place.

What notions such as First or Third World hide are the relations, between nations and between capitals, that lead some economies to develop and others to underdevelop. In other words, for there to be dependent economies and regions, there must be imperialist economies and regions, and vice versa. None can be explained in itself, in isolation, but in the relationship. For this reason, bracketing the United States and Brazil (no matter how successful the efforts of their ruling classes to consolidate themselves as sub-imperialism), on the one hand; or Great Britain and India (the old imperialism together with one of its former and profitable colonies), on the other, and affirming that there are only "differences of degree", is an erroneous formulation from beginning to end. The cases selected help to hide the underlying fallacy, when considering economies that, being distant in terms of "degree", are qualitatively distant from the forms of reproduction of capital that sustain them. In any case, the issue would be clearer if the United States and Honduras, for example, or Great Britain and Nigeria, were pointed out. Here the argument that there are only "degree differences" would no longer be so defensible and would lead one to wonder about the qualitative differences between these economies.

The problem is that in the midst of the deep integration that globalization has encouraged, capital flows move in multiple directions, but when it comes to the distribution of profits, they end up settling in economies of the so-called central world.28 The fact that there are islets of wealth in the dependent world and islets of poverty in the central world do not make the world system today a "muddle" (ah! the fetishism of appearances), where the relations that make some and other particular capitalisms is not only a matter of "degrees" (ah! the old thesis of the stages of development revived), but of differentiated forms of reproduction of capital, as differentiated are the appropriations of value of some to the detriment of others.

Differentiated reproductions of capital

From the above we can say that super-exploitation, as it assumes capitalist exploitation, which implies violation of the value of the labour-power, expands into all corners of the capitalist world system. But this statement should not lead us to forget the *differentiated role* played by its forms in the *reproduction of capital* in the imperialist and central world and in dependent regions and economies.

In the central, imperialist world the predominant forms in times without crisis, are related to the intensification of labour, which is closely linked to the elevation of productivity, and to a lesser extent the prolongation of the working day and the appropriation of the consumption fund, particularly to migrant workers and the hardest hit layers of the working population. Here the exhaustion of the workers has as one of its expressions the illnesses associated with stress and acute and prolonged depression. Higher wages during the useful lifetime of the workers for capital, allows in turn more comfortable incomes for those in retirement. That will be all the greater if the withdrawal is made in economies where the exchange of dollars into local currencies favours holders of dollars. In Mexico, for example, there are cities that have been practically "taken over" by U.S. retirees, such as San Miguel de Allende, in the state of Guanajuato, and to a lesser extent Valle de Bravo, in the state of Mexico.

---

28   Of the 50 largest companies in the world in 2022 by sales, according to Forbes Global 2000, 22 are from the United States (5 among the top 10), 11 from China, 3 from Germany, 3 from France, 3 from the United Kingdom, and 2 from Japan (https://www.forbes.com/lists/global2000/?sh=159332745ac0, 9 February 2023).

What I want to emphasise is that the predominance of this form of super-exploitation does not alter, but reinforces, forms of reproduction of capital where the majority of wage earners, by the amount of their perceptions, play a dynamic role in the realisation of surplus-value and in the internal market. They are important for capital not only as producers but also as consumers. All of this is redefined in situations of global economic crisis, such as the one we have been experiencing at least since 2009 to date. We have already seen that in moments of a substantial fall in the rate of profit, an immediate resource of capital is to resort to super-exploitation. And that is what happens in our day, whether in the dependent world or in the imperial world. The problem that opens up is to ask ourselves what will happen, if capital overcomes this crisis, to the wages and other benefits of the workers in the central world. What can be foreseen is that in any case they will take a long time to recover.

The situation is diametrically distinct when the prevailing form of super-exploitation is directly wages below the value of labour-power (appropriation of the consumption fund), which in turn encourages the prolongation of the workday as a mechanism to achieve extra payments to the insufficient standard daily wage, or the intensification of work, as the only ways to survive. The immediate cost of all this is a premature exhaustion of the workers, their depredation, appropriation of their life fund, without their income allowing them to play a significant role in the internal market and in the realisation of the surplus-value in the years of useful life, and even less in the years of retirement. The reproduction of capital (dynamic, hegemonic, axis of accumulation) creates productive structures that turn their backs on the needs of the producers, and for its realisation opens to foreign markets, creating in turn reduced local markets of high power consumers. Workers importance is then as generators of surplus-value, but not as realisers of that surplus-value, as producers but barely as consumers.

Conclusion

The problem then is *not* in *affirming the universality of super-exploitation*, but in *not distinguishing the specific forms* that predominate in the imperial world and in the dependent world and the *differentiated consequences* that this provokes in the forms of how capital is reproduced, as well as the *differentiated bases that it establishes for the development of the class struggle*.

In spite of minor errors or deficiencies in its formulation, super-exploitation constitutes the axis of a central theoretical proposal to make intelligible the processes and relations that operate in dependent capitalism, in its imbrication with the capitalist world system. To amend Marini's plan in this sense only has significance if it is to broaden the horizon to further open reflections, and not for formal pedantry that leads to making his proposals little more than a dead letter.

References

Carcanholo, Marcelo Dias (2013), "(Im)precisiones acerca de la categoría superexplotación de la fuerza de trabajo", in *Razón y Revolución*, n. 25, Buenos Aires.

Hardt, Michel and Antonio Negri (2000), *Empire*, Cambridge MA/London, Harvard University Press.

Hegel, Georg W. (2010), *The Science of Logic*, translated and edited by George Di Giovanni, Cambridge, Cambridge University Press.

Marcuse, Herbert (1955), *Reason and Revolution: Hegel and the Rise of Social Theory*, 2nd edition, London, Routledge and Kegan Paul.

Marini, Ruy Mauro (2022), *The Dialectics of Dependency*, Monthly Review Press, New York.

Marini, Ruy Mauro (1978), "Las razones del neodesarrollismo", in *Revista Mexicana de Sociología*, Número extraordinario, Instituto de Investigaciones Sociales, UNAM, México, pp. 57-106.

Martins, Carlos Eduardo (2019), *Globalizaçao, dependencia e neoliberalismo na América Latina*, Boitempo Editorial, Sao Paulo.

Marx, Karl (1973), *Grundrisse: Foundations of the Critique of Political Economy (Rough Draft)*, Harmondsworth, Penguin.

Marx, Karl (1976), *Capital. Volume 1*, London/New York, Penguin.

Marx, Karl (1981), *Capital. Volume 3*, London/New York, Penguin.

Osorio, Jaime (2004), *Crítica de la economía vulgar. Reproducción del capital y dependencia*, M. A. Porrúa-UAZ, México.

Osorio, Jaime (2009), *Explotación redoblada y actualidad de la revolución*, Ítaca-UAM-Xochimilco, México.

Osorio, Jaime (2012), "El nuevo patrón exportador de especialización productiva en América Latina", en *Revista da Sociedade Brasileira de Economía Política*, núm. 31, fevereiro 2012, Sao Paulo, pp. 31-63.

Pérez Soto, Carlos (2008), *Desde Hegel. Para una crítica radical de las ciencias sociales*, Itaca, México.

Pérez Soto, Carlos (2010), "Lógica ontológica y lógica formal", en http://grupohege l.blogspot.com/2010/01/logica-ontologica-y-logica-formal.html.

Rosdolsky, Roman (1977), *The Making of Marx's 'Capital'*, London, Pluto Press.

Santi, Paolo (1971 [1965]), "El debate sobre el imperialismo en los clásicos del marxismo", in *Teoría marxista del imperialismo*, Cuadernos de Pasado y Presente n. 10, Córdoba.

Serra, José y F. H. Cardoso "Las desventuras de la dialéctica de la dependencia", en *Revista Mexicana de Sociología*, Número extraordinario, 1978, Instituto de Investigaciones Sociales, UNAM, México.

Sotelo, Adrián (2003), *La reestructuración del mundo del trabajo. Superexplotación y nuevos paradigmas de la organización del trabajo*, Itaca/ENET/Universidad Obrera de México, México.

Sotelo, Adrián (2012), *Los rumbos del trabajo. Superexplotación y precariedad social en el siglo XXI*, Miguel Ángel Porrúa/UNAM, México.

Valenzuela Feijóo, José (1997), "Sobreexplotación y dependencia", *Investigación Económica*, núm. 221, Instituto de Investigaciones Económica, UNAM, México, julio-septiembre.

A review of the Marxist debate on unequal exchange and its relevance as a determination of uneven development in the capitalist world system

Introduction

In recent years there has been a resurgence of interest in Marxist dependency theory as a relevant paradigm for explaining the specificity of capitalism in Latin America. Given the renewed interest in this theory (which is one of the most important contributions of Latin American critical thought to social sciences) it is necessary to critically recover its formulations and discuss its main theses in order to continue investigating the determinations of dependent capitalism and of the uneven development of capitalism as a world system.

Ruy Mauro Marini, the most important author of this theoretical perspective, argued that "the fundamental task of Marxist dependency theory is to determine the *specific laws* by which the dependent economy is governed" (Marini, 2022: 165). In line with this indication, the aim of this chapter is to clarify the determinations of unequal exchange, as well as its implications as one of the fundamental processes that characterise dependent capitalism, by reviewing the Marxist debate on this issue.

At least since David Ricardo's work, one of the most deeply rooted ideas in economic thought is that international trade has positive effects for all countries that participate in it. According to the classical theory of international trade, productive specialisation based on comparative advantages results in mutually beneficial international exchanges for all countries involved. Contrary to the mainstream interpretations, one of the main arguments of Marxist authors who have researched the laws of international trade is that it contributes to the uneven development of capitalism as a world system. Foreign trade is not neutral ground, nor does it spontaneously reduce the diversity of material and social conditions of production in the world system. On the contrary: international trade results in the differentiated appropriation of surplus-value between the countries participating in it,[29] thus giving rise to differentiated conditions of reproduction between imperialist capitalism and dependent capitalism.

It is sometimes claimed that the arguments of Marxist dependency theory on unequal exchange have their most important precedent and influence in the research carried out by Raúl Prebisch and other authors from the Economic Commission for Latin America (ECLAC) on the deterioration in the terms of trade and the "transfer of income" abroad through international trade (Prebisch, 1966; Rodríguez, 2006). However, as argued in this text, the formulations of Marxist dependency theory are a continuation of the long and important reflection that Marxist authors have formulated on international trade as a means of transferring value from dependent countries to imperialist ones. Likewise, Marxist dependency theory makes some relevant contributions to these studies by considering unequal exchange as a fundamental determination for the reproduction of unevenness in the capitalist world system and by researching its impact on the qualitatively different form assumed by the reproduction of Latin American dependent capitalism.

This chapter systematises the main contributions and debates from the critique of political economy on the determinations and dynamics of the transfers of surplus-value in international trade. To do so, it first traces and recovers some of the key arguments formulated in Karl Marx's work to study the laws ruling international trade under capitalism. Second, it presents a brief assessment on the way the theorists of imperialism understood the economic function of foreign trade. Third, it reviews key aspects of the debate on unequal exchange in the 1960s and 1970s. It then analyses Ernest Mandel's and Roman Rosdolsky's contributions to the discussion on unequal exchange, and highlights the contributions of Marxist dependency theory on this subject. Lastly, it closes with concluding remarks.

---

29   In this sense, Guglielmo Carchedi and Michael Roberts (2021: 40) point out that the "appropriation of surplus value [is] inherent in trade".

Preliminary clarifications

Before beginning the discussion on unequal exchange, it is necessary to formulate some theoretical and methodological issues.

On the level of abstraction and the unit of analysis

The study of dependency and its fundamental determinations (one of which is unequal exchange) has as its starting point the analysis of "capital in general" proposed by Marx in *Capital*, but it does not stop there. On the contrary: it requires incorporating additional determinations and relations into the analysis to account for the differentiated forms of reproduction of capital in the world system. Some of these are: the deployment of "many capitals" in the world market; the consideration of the state as a synthesis of social relations and condensation of political power; the existence of multiple states with varying degrees of sovereignty; the exercise of asymmetrical relations of power and appropriation between states and capitals; the international division of labour; and competition and exchange relations between capitals and spheres of production based in different states. Consequently, research on dependency—and on imperialism—is framed within the study of the development of capitalism as a world system, which Marx proposed as the culmination of his unfinished critique of political economy.

As argued here, unequal exchange results from differences in the composition of capital and in the rate of exploitation between capitals and spheres of production located in different countries. For the purposes of this chapter, "imperialist countries" are those where there is a persistent concentration of capitals and spheres of production which incorporate more advanced technological development and which, consequently, have a higher average productivity and higher composition of capital. Due to these circumstances, they permanently receive positive net flows of surplus-value, exploited by the capitals located in the dependent countries. On the other hand, "dependent countries" are those where capital and spheres of production with lower technological development, lower productivity and lower composition of capital are concentrated. Under these circumstances, capitals and spheres of production in these countries systematically transfer surplus-value to those located in the imperialist countries. It should be stressed that these are transfers of surplus-value between capitals and spheres of production located in different national spaces, not transfers between countries *per se*. If the transfers of surplus-value through unequal exchange *appear* as transfers between countries, it is a result of the hierarchical and asymmetrical international division of labour characteristic of imperialism, which conditions the heterogeneous and polarised distribution of the productive forces in the world system.

Although this text is not intended to deal extensively with the relevance of the state for uneven development in the world system, it is important to make some general notes on the subject.30 State action is of great significance in explaining the existence of heterogeneous forms of capitalism and the reasons for polarisation in the development of the productive forces. Capitals and spheres of production are located in specific national spaces, where particular economic and political conditions prevail. While it is true that capitalism is a world system, it is not a homogeneous unit. On the contrary: world capitalism is a complex system characterised by national and regional inequalities, as well as by a hierarchical structure among the different elements that make it up (capitals, industries, nations). This heterogeneity is determined to an important extent by the existence of nation-states, which, by giving rise to national differences in wages and taxes, by actively encouraging the accumulation of capital in certain strategic sectors, by promoting scientific and technological development, etc., impact the conditions for capital reproduction.

The "strength" of capitals and the strength of the states where they are headquartered condition each other. The action of the state conditions the development of capitals and their centralisation in certain geographical areas. States serve as lever and support for the conditions that allow for the accumulation of the capitals settled in them.31 Since the most innovative

---

30   Relevant formulations on the centrality of the state for the reproduction of the world system's heterogeneity can be found in Osorio (2014a, 2017).

31   "Nation states operate as a point of reference and central support for capitals" (Osorio, 2017: 21).

and technologically advanced production processes depend on the stimulus and protection of "strong" states, a geographical consequence of capital accumulation on a world scale is that the most developed capitals and branches of production tend to be located or clustered in a handful of states.

Different types of transfers of surplus-value

There are different types of transfers of surplus-value from dependent countries to imperialist ones. One of them, addressed in this chapter, is that which takes place in international trade, known as "unequal exchange". But it is not the only one: broadly speaking, there are three types of international transfers of surplus-value, related to each of the cycles of capital (money capital, productive capital and commodity capital), as well as its different forms (industrial capital, commercial capital and interest-bearing capital).

As will be explained at length below, unequal exchange results from the operation of the law of value in the world market due to differentials in the composition of capital and in the rate of surplus-value between the capitals and spheres of production involved in foreign trade. On the other hand, the export of capital or foreign direct investment—which was considered by Lenin as one of the most important characteristics of imperialism—gives rise to another type of international transfers of surplus-value. Through foreign direct investment, the firms of a country produce commodities abroad, so that they participate directly in the production of surplus-value and the exploitation of workers outside the country where they are based. In this case, the transfer of the exploited surplus-value to the countries of origin of the transnational firms takes place by means of profit repatriation, etc. A third type of transfer of surplus-value from dependent countries to imperialist ones corresponds to interest-bearing capital: the payment of interest on public debt or on government bonds and the amortisation of bank loans, among others.

The aforementioned types of international transfers of surplus-value do not exist independently of each other but are articulated and feed back on each other. The relative weight and importance of the different types of transfers is modified in the different stages of capitalist development and according to the particular conditions of each social formation.32 The particularity of the different forms of domination and expropriation in the capitalist world system lies, to a large extent, in which is the predominant type of transfer and appropriation of surplus-value by the capitals based in the imperialist countries. The study of concrete and historically determined situations requires looking at how the different types of transfers of surplus-value are organised and intertwined.

An important conclusion to be drawn from the above is that imperialist domination over dependent countries is much more complex than unequal exchange and is irreducible to it. Consequently, unequal exchange is a fundamental determination of dependency and uneven development in the world system, but it is far from being the only one.

The study of the other types of transfers of surplus-value is beyond the scope of this chapter. Unravelling the complexity of capitalist domination in the world system requires a detailed study of the different forms of transfers of surplus-value, their articulation and feedback, as well as the way in which they contribute to produce what David Harvey (2006) calls an "uneven geographical development" of capitalism. In this chapter, the study is limited to the foundations and dynamics of a particular type of transfers of surplus-value: the one originating in international trade, known as unequal exchange.

Clarifications on "unequal exchange"

The concept of "unequal exchange" is part of a long tradition of critical Marxism that has investigated the laws governing international trade and the causes of the unevenness of capitalism as a world system. Many authors—among them Henryk Grossman (1992), Roman Rosdolsky (1977), Ernest Mandel (1998) and Ruy Mauro Marini (2022)—have used this term to describe the process by which a country obtains, in exchange for the product of one hour of labour, commodities whose production has required more labour time in other countries.

---

32   See Mandel (1998).

From the controversial and influential intervention of Arghiri Emmanuel (1972) to the debate on international trade, the notion of unequal exchange acquired problematic theoretical and political implications from a Marxist perspective. Consequently, the difficulties stemming from the way Emmanuel used this concept need to be identified and clarified in order to be able to speak of unequal exchange without being misleading.

As understood in this text, unequal exchange is not a phenomenon exclusive to the sphere of circulation. On the contrary: this type of transfer of surplus-value reveals the complexity of capitalist reproduction as a unit of production and circulation. Unequal exchange implies a redistribution and differentiated appropriation of surplus-value in the circulation of commodities, but whose basis lies in the heterogeneity of the material and social conditions of production between capitals, branches of production and nations.

On the other hand, the transfers of surplus-value in international trade commonly called unequal exchange are a result of the validity of the law of value in the world market, not a consequence of its violation or transgression. This does not mean, that in the capitalist economy there are no violations of the law of value or plundering of some nations by others, but it is important to note that unequal exchange exists independently of such violations or plunder.

Additionally, by pointing out that unequal exchange consists of transfers of *surplus-value,* it is underscored that the fundamental contradiction of capitalism as a world system is the exploitation of workers by capital, not an alleged contradiction between "rich" and "poor" countries, as Emmanuel claimed.33

In sum, unequal exchange is not exclusive to the sphere of circulation; it is a transfer (redistribution) of surplus-value produced in geographical spaces with uneven material and social conditions of production,

---

33 Emmanuel's arguments about the "exploitation" of poor nations by rich ones "lead to relations between classes being made to appear as simple 'relations between countries,' that is, to replacing the real antagonism between workers and exploiters by the fictitious one between 'rich nations' and 'poor nations.'" (Bettelheim, 1972: 310).

which reveals the complexity of capitalist reproduction as a unit of production and circulation. Understanding unequal exchange as a particular type of transfer of *surplus-value* accounts for the pre-eminence of the exploitation of workers (since a *transfer* of surplus-value presupposes the *production* of surplus-value) and for the centrality of class antagonism in the capitalist world system. It is in this sense that the concept of unequal exchange is used here.

It is necessary to add, lastly, that even when transfers of surplus-value in international trade do not represent a violation of the law of value in the world market, the formalism of equivalence in exchanges conceals a relation of appropriation of value based on uneven material and social conditions of production, on qualitatively different forms of participation in the international division of labour, on secular colonial legacies that acquire concreteness in heterogeneous forms of reproduction of capital, on differential relations of power and sovereignty, etc.

On the concept of "composition of capital"

It is important to note some issues regarding the concept of "composition of capital" and its use for the analysis of international trade. Authors such as David Harvey (2006) and Ben Fine and Alfredo Saad-Filho (2010) have pointed out that in Marxist literature the differences between the concepts of "value-composition" and "organic composition of capital" are often not established and they are even treated as synonyms. In the analysis of international trade, it is relevant to note a difference between them, resulting from the national differences in wages and in the rates of surplus-value. In volume one of *Capital*, Marx defined the composition of capital as follows:

> The composition of capital is to be understood in a twofold sense. As value, it is determined by the proportion in which it is divided into constant capital, or the value of the means of production, and variable capital, or the value of labour-power, the sum total of wages. As material, as it functions in the process of production, all capital is divided into means of production and living labour-power. This latter composition is determined by the relation between the mass of the means of production employed on the one hand, and the mass of labour necessary for their employment on the other. I call the former the value-composition, the latter the technical composition of capital. There is a close correlation between the two. To express this, I call the value-composition of capital, in so far as it is determined by its

technical composition and mirrors the changes in the latter, the organic composition of capital. (Marx, 1992: 762)

In this passage, it is clear that Marx used *organic* composition of capital to refer to a particular type of change in the value-composition of capital: variations in the value-composition of capital insofar as they result from changes in technological conditions of production and reflect them. An implicit assumption of the concept of organic composition of capital in Marx's work is that the wage and the rate of surplus-value are constant within a country in a particular period, so at a given wage the investment on variable capital can be seen as an index of the quantity of living labour set in motion by a given capital.34

The situation is different when dealing with the composition of capital between nations. In the world market, capitals with similar technological conditions operate, but as they settle in different countries, they pay different wages and have different rates of exploitation.35 Consider a situation in which the technical composition of capital is identical between two firms operating in the same sphere of production but in two countries with different wage-levels (a car assembly plant with the same technologies in the United States and in Mexico, for example). In this case, each worker puts into motion proportionally the same mass of means of production (machinery, inputs, etc.). As material, the objective and subjective components of the process of production are the same. However, their expression in terms of value is different because of the national differences in wages (wages in Mexico are lower than in the United States).36 Thus, the value of

---

34   "Since we also assume that the rate of surplus-value and the working day are constant and since this assumption also involves constancy of wages, a certain quantity of variable capital means a certain quantity of labour-power set in motion and hence a certain quantity of labour objectifying itself" (Marx, 1993a: 243).

35   In addition to their importance for unequal exchange, national differences in wages have an enormous relevance as a source of surplus profits for foreign direct investment of companies from imperialist countries into dependent ones.

36   According to the ECLAC (2017: 167), hourly wages paid in the automotive industry in Mexico are 10 times lower than those paid to workers in the United States in the same industry.

the ratio $\frac{c}{v}$ differs between the firms operating in both countries because of the different investment in variable capital they made by purchasing the same mass of labour-power, even though the material and technical content of the process of production is the same. In these cases, since the differences in the value-composition of capital are not determined by changes in the technical composition but are the result of differences in the price paid for labour-power between countries, one cannot speak of different *organic* compositions of capital in the strict sense of the term. As can be seen, it is important to distinguish between the concepts of *technical, organic* and *value composition* of capital when considering the existence of multiple capitals, branches and countries that compete in the world market. Considering this, in the study of the formation of prices of production in international trade and unequal exchange it is more accurate to speak of the value-composition of capitals.37 Therefore, by "composition of capital" this text refers to the value-composition of capital, unless otherwise stated.

Having clarified these points, let us now consider and analyse the main arguments and debates from the critique of political economy on the transfer of surplus-value in international trade.

Keys in Marx's work on unequal exchange

The dynamics and trends of international trade were not systematically presented by Marx in *Capital* or in any of the books he published during his lifetime. Marx did not incorporate this subject in *Capital* because its

---

37 This is similar to Marx's point about the possibility of the value-composition of two capitals diverging because of the differences in value between the raw materials used, even though their technical compositions are identical: "Certain operations in copper or iron, for example, may involve the same proportion between labour-power and means of production. But because copper is dearer than iron, the value relationship between variable and constant capital will be different in each case, and so therefore will the value composition of the two capitals taken as a whole. The distinction between technical composition and value composition shows itself in every branch of industry by the way the value ratio between the two portions of capital may change while the technical composition remains constant, whereas, with a changed technical composition, the value ratio may remain the same" (Marx, 1993a: 244-245).

inclusion was beyond the limits he had drawn for that book. Although he did not deal extensively with the subject, in various passages of *Capital* and the *Grundrisse* Marx gave elements for its further research. From these passages in his works, as well as from the contributions of later authors, there are elements to systematically formulate a theoretical approach to the transfers of surplus-value that have been called unequal exchange.

Marx was very clear about the limits within which, for theoretical and methodological reasons, his *magnum opus* lay. Let us recall that the book on "capital" was the first of six that Marx intended to write in his project of the *critique of political economy*, while the book on the "world market"— which he considered "the very basis and living atmosphere of the capitalist mode of production" (Marx, 1993a: 205)—was the sixth and last of his original outline. A passage at the beginning of part two of volume three of *Capital*, which deals with the formation of a general rate of profit, gives an account of the strict limits that Marx himself imposed on his research:

> The distinctions between rates of surplus-value in different countries and hence between the different national levels of exploitation of labour are completely outside the scope of our present investigation. The object of this Part is simply to present the way in which a general rate of profit is arrived at within one particular country. (Marx, 1993a: 242)

However, although Marx explicitly stated that he would not consider the different rates of surplus-value between nations because to do so would be beyond the scope of his investigation, he later provided relevant elements to address the question of the formation of the general rate of profit in the world market:

> It is clear for all, however, that in comparing different national rates of profit one need only combine what has been developed earlier with the arguments to be developed here [in part two of volume three of *Capital*, "The Transformation of Profit into Average Profit"]. One would first consider the variation between national rates of surplus-value and then compare, on the basis of these given rates of surplus-value, how national rates of profit differ. In so far as their variation is not the result of variation in the national rates of surplus-value, it must be due to circumstances in

which, as in this chapter, surplus-value is assumed to be everywhere the same, to be constant. (Marx, 1993a: 242)38

It is then a matter of recovering the keys presented by Marx and extending his approaches to the formation of a general rate of profit "within one particular country" to the study of international trade—the systematic investigation of which would be dealt with in the fifth book of the original outline of Marx's critique of political economy.39

In the production of commodities for international trade, two processes occur simultaneously: 1) the formation of the world value of commodities within the same branch of production and 2) the redistribution of the surplus-value socially produced among different branches through the formation of a general rate of profit.40 Both processes result from the validity of the law of value as the regulating principle of social reproduction in the capitalist mode of production.

In the former, capitals in different countries produce the same type of commodity for international trade and employ very different labour times in its production. Competition leads to the formation of a socially necessary labour time to produce that commodity in the international

---

38 From what Marx has said here, a question of significant importance for the study of unequal exchange can be deduced, which will be dealt with later: there are two causes that give rise to the inequality of rates of profit between nations. These are: 1) the variations in the national rates of surplus-value and 2) the differences in the composition of capital (to which Marx refers in this passage when he speaks of "the arguments to be developed here", "in this chapter" [chapter 8, "Different Compositions of Capital in Different Branches of Production, and the Resulting Variation in Rates of Profit"]).

39 In 1857 Marx described the original plan of his 'critique of political economy', which remained unfinished. In this original outline and in its later versions, Marx structured his work into six "books": "I examine the system of bourgeois economy in the following order: *capital, landed property, wage-labour; the State, foreign trade, world market*" (Marx, 1977).

40 It is worth noting briefly what Marx understood by "branch" or "sphere" of production. In *Grundrisse*, Marx stated: "production is always a *particular* branch of production— e.g. agriculture, cattle-raising, manufactures etc.—or it is a *totality*" (Marx, 1993b: 86). In the same sense, in *Capital* (volume one, chapter 14, "The Division of Labour and Manufacture") he related the existence of different branches of production to the division of labour within a society. The social division of labour implies the existence of different branches of production, in which use-values of different types are produced and concrete work of different kinds is carried out.

space; as value is established in the international space, capitals with a higher productivity for the production of that particular type of commodity produce extraordinary surplus-value and obtain a higher value in international trade.

In the latter, when commodities from different branches of production are exchanged in international trade, there is a transfer of surplus-value from branches with low composition of capital to others with high capital composition, so that the rate of profit equalises among the branches "under the pressure of competition" (Marx, 1993a: 274). The formation of value in the international space and the redistribution of surplus-value through the equalisation of profit rates occur in the circulation of commodities under the pressure of competition and have their basis in the inequality of the material and social conditions of production between capitals and branches of production.

In both cases, commodities are exchanged whose production has required unequal quantities of labour. In both cases, capitals and branches of industry with high composition of capital and higher productivity, located in imperialist countries, appropriate more value than they produced, and capitals and spheres with low composition of capital and lower productivity located in the dependent countries appropriate less value.

There are different passages in *Capital* in which Marx addresses the circumstances that make the transfer of surplus-value in international trade possible.

Let us first deal with the case of *commodities of the same type* produced in different countries. In one of the first passages in which he discusses this, in part six of volume one of *Capital*, he points to the possibility that commodities of the same type can be exchanged for prices that differ from their national values. "The different quantities of commodities of the same kind, produced in different countries in the same working time, have ... unequal international values, which are expressed in different prices, *i.e.* in sums of money varying according to international values" (Marx, 1992: 702). The international value of commodities differs from their value in the national spaces in which they were produced.41 "On the world market, national labour which is more productive also counts as more intensive"; "the more intense national labour ... produces in the same time more value, which expresses itself in more money" (Marx, 1992: 702).

Why is it that in international trade commodities of the same type are not exchanged for their individual or national values? The value of commodities produced in different countries differ because they have been produced under dissimilar material and social conditions. In the capitalist world system, capitals and countries have different levels of development of productive forces and, therefore, *different levels of labour productivity and intensity*. In these circumstances, socially necessary labour time to produce commodities of the same type differs between countries. The same is true of the surplus-value contained in commodities produced in different countries. Since commodities have been produced under individual and national conditions in which the composition of capital, the rate of exploitation, etc., are different, they will represent very different magnitudes of value in their respective national spaces.

Nevertheless, within a branch of production competition tends to equalise the values of commodities: although they have been produced under substantially different conditions, commodities of the same kind produced for foreign trade are sold at the same value (for in general, and under the pressure of competition, use-values of the same kind and of homogeneous quality must be sold at the same value, even though they were produced under very dissimilar conditions).42 For this to happen,

---

41   In this regard, Marx explicitly spoke of "the separation between the internal or national spheres of commodity circulation and its universal sphere, the world market" (Marx, 1992: 222). The existence of different spheres of commodity circulation highlights a significant fact: in its development, the capitalist mode of production has a complex structure, which is at once national and global. In this regard, see Osorio (2017).

42   "The concept of market price means that the same price is paid for all commodities of the same kind, even if these are produced under very different individual conditions and may therefore have very different cost prices" (Marx, 1993a: 300). Also: "the fact that commodities of the same kind have an identical market price is the way in which the social character of value is realized on the basis of the capitalist mode of production" (Marx, 1993a: 800).

commodities produced under the most diverse productivities and intensities of labour will have to be reduced to a new socially necessary labour
time on the world sphere, which will determine their magnitude of world
value.[43]

In the case of commodities produced in *different branches of industry*
and in different countries for international trade, the diversity of magnitudes of value and surplus-value will be multiplied and proportionate to
the existing variety of levels of productivity of labour, intensities of labour,
compositions of capital, national rates of exploitation, etc. Within each
branch of production, as stated above, the different values are reduced to
a new magnitude of value in the world sphere, representing the socially
necessary labour time required to produce *that kind* of commodity in the
world system, in such a way that they "develop their value universally".

However, even if the commodities produced in different branches of
industry were exchanged *at their values* in the world market (and thus express the socially necessary labour time for their production in the world
sphere), there would be—analogous to what happens within a national
sphere—multiple rates of profit among the different branches of production. This would pose a problem, since it would imply that branches with
a low composition of capital would obtain a higher rate of profit than
branches with a high composition of capital, since the former put into motion a greater quantity of living labour—the only source of value and surplus-value—and of surplus labour than the latter. However, just as within
a country, in international trade "no such variation in the average rate of
profit exists between different branches of industry, and it could not exist
without abolishing the entire system of capitalist production" (Marx,
1993a: 252). Therefore, it is necessary to move on to the analysis of the
exchange of commodities at their price of production in international
trade.[44]

---

43   "In world trade, commodities develop their value universally" (Marx, 1992: 240).
44   It should be explicitly noted that this is not about two different and contradictory laws
      of value, but of the same law of value at different levels of abstraction, since the price of
      production is a form of value. As Bettelheim argues, "the law of value functions as the

Before addressing comprehensively the formation of prices of production in international trade, let us look at a couple more passages in which Marx formulates relevant elements to develop the question.

In the part one of volume three of *Capital*, Marx states that in addition to the different profit rates between branches of production within a country, there is a wide diversity of rates of profit between countries: "we thus obtain various sets of cases [of rates or profit] which we can consider … as different capitals, existing simultaneously alongside one another, and brought in for purposes of comparison, *e.g.* from different branches of industry or from different countries" (Marx, 1993a: 145). The existence of different national rates of profit is due to the fact that the degree of technological development and the average composition of capitals and branches of production differ between countries.

The *Grundrisse* contains the following passage, which is clearer in relation to this point:

> From the possibility that profit may be less than surplus value, hence that capital [may] exchange profitably without realizing itself in the strict sense, it follows that not only individual capitalists, but also nations may continually exchange with one another, may even continually repeat the exchange on an ever-expanding scale, without for that reason necessarily gaining in equal degrees. One of the nations may continually appropriate for itself a part of the surplus labour of the other, giving back nothing for it in the exchange (Marx, 1993b: 872).

Here, Marx goes beyond what he states in *Capital* and points out that when nations exchange with one another they may obtain profits which differ from the surplus-value produced within themselves and consequently may appropriate rates and masses of profit different from those which they would have obtained if the commodities had been sold within their respective national frontiers. In addition, he clearly points out that one of the

---

law of the formation of prices of production, the law that actually regulates the social process of reproduction" (Bettelheim, 1972: 281). Under fully developed commodity production, "there is no 'other' value that is more 'authentic' than price of production" (Bettelheim, 1972: 277).

nations "may continually appropriate for itself a part of the surplus labour of the other".

From these extracts of Marx's works, as well as from some others to which reference will be made later, it follows that in international trade commodities are exchanged for prices differing from their national values; in this process, some nations persistently transfer surplus-value to others without getting anything back in the exchange. These transfers of surplus-value result from the tendency towards the formation of an average rate of profit in international trade. For those capitals, branches of production and nations which in this way obtain a higher rate of profit than they would have if their commodities had been sold within their national frontiers, this higher rate of profit implies the *appropriation of* a part of the surplus-labour produced in other capitals, branches or nations; on the other hand, for those capitals, branches and nations which through international trade realise a lower rate of profit than they would have obtained by the sale of their commodities within their national frontiers, this lower rate of profit implies an *unfavourable transfer of surplus-value.*

Those capitals, branches and countries which continuously appropriate a part of the surplus-labour and surplus-value produced in others can do so because they have incorporated better technologies, have a higher composition of capital and a higher productivity of labour; those which transfer a part of the surplus-value exploited in them suffer this drain of surplus-value because their material and social conditions of production are less developed in capitalist terms. The basis of these transfers of surplus-value in international trade is the inequality in the material and social conditions of production in the capitalist world system: the uneven development of the productive forces, as well as the differentials in the composition of capital, productivity of labour and rates of surplus-value between capitals, branches and nations.

Let us now consider the formation of prices of production in international trade.45 As has been pointed out, if in foreign trade commodities
were sold at their values or at their national prices of production, there
would be a multitude of rates of profit. If commodities were sold at their
values, branches of production with a higher composition of capital would
obtain lower rates of profit than those with a lower composition of capital.
If this were the case, the branches that incorporate a higher technological
development would be "punished" with a lower rate of profit; thus, the
conditions for the accumulation of capital and for capitalist technological
change would be undermined. This would be contradictory to the dynamics of the capitalist mode of production, whose basic logic consists of the
pursuit for extra surplus-value and surplus profit through technological
change in order to raise productivity. On the other hand, if commodities
were sold according to their *national* prices of production, capitals and
branches of production based in imperialist countries would obtain a
lower rate of profit in international trade than those located in dependent
countries. On the contrary: in international trade there is a *redistribution*
of the surplus-value socially produced by the capitals and branches based
in different countries through the formation of a general rate of profit. One
of the most relevant implications of this process is that foreign trade is a
counteracting factor of the tendential fall in the rate of profit (Marx,
1993a).

It is relevant to bear in mind that the formation of the general rate of
profit evidences that "the reproduction and valorisation of each individual
capital and of each branch of production is mediated by the reproduction
and valorisation of capital as a whole". Therefore, transfers of surplus-
value must be seen "as the condition of possibility of the reproduction and

---

45 The debate on the formation of prices of production and the so-called "transformation
problem" is wide-ranging and references are vast. For a critical review of the classical
discussions on the "transformation problem", see Ernest Mandel's (1993) introduction
to volume three of *Capital*, as well as the influential article by Anwar Shaikh (1977). For
contemporary debates, see the books edited by Alan Freeman and Guglielmo Carchedi
(1995), Alan Freeman, Andrew Kliman and Julian Wells (2004), as well as the recent
book by Fred Moseley (2016), among others.

valorisation of the total social capital and, therefore, as the condition of possibility of the reproduction and valorisation of its parts in the only way in which this is possible: as a mutually complementary uneven development" (Bartra, 2006: 94-95). Transfers of surplus-value are necessary for the reproduction of capital as a whole, at the same time as they reproduce the inequalities of the parts that make up that whole.

In the capitalist world system there exists a multitude of capitals, branches and nations with different technical and value composition of capitals. These capitals, which incorporate living labour and means of production in the most diverse proportions, produce magnitudes of surplus-value and therefore magnitudes of profit which are originally very different.46 However, despite the fact that the rates of profit originally differ significantly,

> These different rates of profit are balanced out by competition to give a general rate of profit which is the average of all these different rates. The profit that falls to a capital of given size according to this general rate of profit, whatever its organic composition might be, we call the average profit. (Marx, 1993a: 257)47
>
> What competition brings about, first of all in one sphere, is the establishment of a uniform market value and market price out of the various individual values of commodities. But it is only the competition of capitals in *different* spheres that brings forth the production price that equalises the rates of profit between those spheres. (Marx, 1993a: 281)

Competition tends to equalise the rates of profit of the different branches of production participating in international trade at an average rate of profit.

In short, *within a branch* of production, competition leads to the establishment of a uniform market value and a uniform market price for commodities of the same kind, even when the individual conditions under

---

46   "As a result of the differing organic composition of capitals applied in different branches of production ... the rates of profit prevailing in the different branches of production are accordingly originally very different" (Marx, 1993a: 257).

47   Marx's argument in this passage can be applied to the formation of the general rate of profit in international trade, provided that some clarifications—formulated below—are made.

which they were produced and their cost prices differ significantly. On the other hand, *between different branches of production*, competition leads to the formation of a general rate of profit, since each branch of production must obtain—independently of how much surplus-value it exploited directly and of what its composition of capital was—a share of the total surplus-value which is proportional to its own magnitude with respect to total social capital (in this case, of capitals *competing in international trade*).48 Thus, to the cost price of the average producers of the various branches of industry is added the general rate of profit in international trade, so that the average capitals of the various branches realise their international prices of production.

The study of the formation of the general rate of profit in international trade does not cancel but instead complements, from a totality perspective, the analysis of the formation of the general rate of profit within a country, since both represent different but complementary moments and scales of the law of value and the unfolding of the capitalist world system. It is only through the synthesis of those scales that the general movement of the system can be understood.

Two conditions are necessary for the equalisation of the rates of profit: 1) the mobility of capital from one sphere and one place to others and 2) the mobility of labour-power from one branch of production to another and between geographical spaces (Marx, 1993a: 298). The greater the

---

48   Not all capitals participate in the formation of international prices of production: only those that compete in international trade do. According to Marx, competition establishes a market value within a branch of production and equalises the rates of profit between branches of production. Only in competition in the world market do commodities produced under the most diverse conditions "develop their value universally" and effectively become parts of abstract social labour in the world sphere. Although *national* rates of profit are relevant and express the level of the composition of capital and the rate of exploitation within nations, they do not determine the average rate of profit in international trade, since not all capitals operating within countries participate in competition on a world scale. Therefore, the formation of an average rate of profit in international trade does not imply, as Mandel (1998) asserted, the disappearance of the various *national* rates of profit through their generalised levelling. The tendency towards the equalisation of rates of profit in international trade coexists with the diversity of national rates of profit.

mobility, the more quickly this equalisation is accomplished. In the world system, the mobility of capital and labour-power encounter greater obstacles than within a country due to the existence of national frontiers, the difficulties related to means of communication and transport, etc. However, although the international mobility of capital and labour-power is more limited than within a country, it operates effectively and has intensified with the development of capitalism as a world system.49 For these reasons, the average rate of profit in international trade does not exist as a datum, but operates as a tendency. Nevertheless, two things must be kept in mind: 1) that "with the whole of capitalist production, it is always only in a very intricate and approximate way, as an average of perpetual fluctuations which can never be firmly fixed, that the general law prevails as the dominant tendency" (Marx, 1993a: 261); 2) that the characteristic tendencies of capitalism manifest themselves more and more markedly "the more the capitalist mode of production is developed and the less it is adulterated by survivals of earlier economic conditions with which it is amalgamated" (Marx, 1993a: 275), which in this case implies that the tendency towards the formation of the general rate of profit in international trade becomes more pronounced the more the capitalist mode of production develops and the more capitalist relations of production become dominant in the world.50

---

49 For example, the export of capital—whose importance has grown since the phase of classical imperialism described by Lenin (1937)—is a form of the international mobility of capital and has been a crucial element of the expansion of capitalism during the last century. During the so-called "globalisation", the international mobility of capital, commodities and labour-power has acquired an unprecedented magnitude, as has worldwide intercapitalist competition. Far from denying the validity of the law of value in the world market, this ratifies it.

50 In this sense, Charles Bettelheim considered that, when commodities produced within capitalist relations of production are exchanged in international trade, price formation is ruled by the equalisation of the rate of profit between industrial branches: in "the worldwide capitalist system ... the 'formula' of the price of production may appear to constitute the 'rule' for the formation of the prices ... when the exchanges involve commodities all of which are produced within the scope of capitalist production relations" (Bettelheim, 1972: 313-314).

With the formation of the general rate of profit, capitals with average composition within each sphere of production that participate in international trade receive from circulation their cost price but do not appropriate the mass of surplus-value they produced in their own sphere—unless by chance their composition of capital coincides with that of the average social capital. What these capitals realise "is only the surplus-value and hence profit that falls to the share of each aliquot part of the total social capital [in this case, of the social capital that participates in international trade], when evenly distributed, from the total social surplus-value or profit produced in a given time by the social capital in all spheres of production" (Marx, 1993a: 258). Thus, in international trade, and under the pressure of competition, all branches of production tend to realise a general rate of profit when they sell their commodities, not the magnitude of surplus-value they directly exploited. The divergence between the surplus-value produced and the profit appropriated is a condition for the reproduction of capital as a whole and for the realisation of the total surplus-value produced.

Let us now consider in greater detail the surplus profit in foreign trade. At the beginning of his study of the formation of the average rate of profit, Marx pointed out that

> For this whole investigation, when we speak of the composition or the turnover of capital in a specific branch of production, it should be clear enough that we always mean the normal, average situation for capital invested in this branch of production, and refer always to the average of the total capital in the sphere in question, not to chance differences between individual capitals invested there. (Marx, 1993a: 243)

However, when studying surplus profit, one must consider not only the average composition of capital in a specific branch, but also the deviations from the average. Although in the formation of prices of production the rates of profit tend to equalise between spheres, within a sphere the general rate of profit is only effectively realised by capitals whose composition coincides with the average composition of that sphere. Capitals whose composition is above the average of the sphere, by producing under better technological conditions (the cost price of their commodities is below the average, but can be sold for the price of production prevailing in the whole sphere) have the possibility of realising a profit above the average, a surplus profit. The opposite happens with capitals whose composition is below the average within the sphere. Thus, "price of production involves a surplus profit for those producing under the best conditions in any particular sphere of production" (Marx, 1993a: 300).

Marx also points out that the realisation of excess profit above the average is due to the deployment of "exceptional overwork" or "exceptional productivity" in the labour applied:

> In actual fact, the particular interest that one capitalist or capital in a particular sphere of production has in exploiting the workers he directly employs is confined to the possibility of taking an extra cut, making an excess profit over and above the average, either by exceptional overwork, by reducing wages below the average, or by exceptional productivity in the labour applied. (Marx, 1993a: 299)

In the passage quoted, Marx points to three sources of surplus profit: the exceptional productivity of labour applied, the lowering of wages below the average and "exceptional overwork". The first of these sources is generally linked to technological change, to a greater development of the productive forces and to a higher composition of capital. In this case, the individual firm that makes use of cutting-edge technology valorises "the specifically higher productivity of the labour he employs as surplus labour" (Marx, 1993a: 345). This "exceptionally productive labour"[51] results in the production of extra surplus-value, which is the direct source of surplus profit.[52] The second of these sources, the reduction of wages below the average—which, beyond the analysis of "capital in general", could refer to the reduction of wages below the value of labour-power, that is, to the super-

---

51   "The exceptionally productive labour acts as intensified labour; it creates in equal periods of time greater values than average social labour of the same kind" (Marx, 1992: 435).

52   In relation to this, Marx adds: "The specific productivity of labour in one particular sphere, or in one individual business in this sphere, concerns the capitalists directly involved in it only in so far as it enables this particular sphere to make an extra profit in relation to the total capital, or the individual capitalist in relation to his sphere" (Marx, 1993a: 300).

exploitation of labour-power (Marini, 2022)—constitutes an expropria-tion of the workers' consumption fund in order to convert it into a fund for capital accumulation. The third of these sources, "exceptional over-work", can be achieved either through the prolongation of the working day or through intensification of labour; in either case, it implies a greater wear-and-tear of labour-power and a higher degree of exploitation. These sources of surplus profit can occur jointly, intertwining and conjugating.

When studying surplus profits in international trade, it is important to point out some additional considerations with respect to what happens with surplus profit within a branch of production in a country. Within a particular sphere of production, only those capitals which at a given mo-ment produce under the best conditions obtain surplus profits. For indi-vidual firms, the appropriation of surplus profits is transitory: they only temporarily hold the privilege of appropriating surplus profits while the most efficient or superior technologies are generalised. When the once-exceptional methods of production generalise, capitals obtain the average rate of profit. On the other hand, in international trade, surplus profits tend to be systematically appropriated by firms based in the imperialist countries—even if the individual capitals that temporarily realise the sur-plus profit change over time. This is due to the existence of an asymmet-rical and hierarchical international division of labour, in which the spheres of production and capitals with the highest composition of capital, which drive technological change, tend to concentrate in the imperialist coun-tries. In other words, the harvest of surplus profits may be temporary for individual capitals, but it is persistent for those countries where the spheres of production and individual capitals that are at the forefront of techno-logical development are concentrated.

In sum: all branches of production tend to receive the general rate of profit, but only those whose capital composition coincides with the aver-age composition of total social capital sell their commodities for prices proportionate to their value and realise profits equivalent to the surplus-value they originally exploited. The branches or production with high composition of capital appropriate through circulation, in the form of profit, more surplus-value than they themselves exploited. The opposite happens with the branches with low composition of capital, which receive from circulation less profit than the surplus-value they exploited and *transfer surplus-value* to those with above-average composition of capital. Since in the capitalist world system there is an asymmetrical international division of labour and a heterogeneous geographical distribution of technological development, branches of production with high composition of capital tend to concentrate in the imperialist countries—the production of cutting-edge means of production is a relevant example. As a result, imperialist countries tend to *persistently appropriate* surplus-value through international trade. On the other hand, branches with lower composition of capital tend to concentrate in the dependent countries, which leads to a constant transfer of surplus-value to imperialist ones. Simultaneously, within each branch, the capitals with the improved methods of production and higher productivity—which also tend to be located in imperialist countries—produce their commodities with an individual cost price lower than the average, which allows them to appropriate surplus profits in the sale of their commodities for their production price.

The differentiated appropriation of surplus-value through international trade implies an increase in the absolute magnitude of surplus-value that imperialist countries realise and can accumulate, as well as a reduction of realised surplus-value and, consequently, a restriction of accumulation for the dependent countries. This generates differentiated forms of reproduction of capital, which tend to reinforce the development of the former and the underdevelopment and dependency of the latter.

At the basis of unequal exchange is the imperialist division of labour. Although a detailed analysis of the different historical configurations of the international division of labour lies beyond the scope of this text, some general considerations can be made. The subordinate position of the dependent countries in the international division of labour has its origin in their colonial history and was consolidated in the 19th century, when the industrial revolution in Western European countries flooded the markets of the colonies and the dependent countries. The industrial revolution ruined handicraft production and stifled the incipient endogenous processes of capital accumulation in those regions, forcing them to become suppliers of raw materials and food for the colonial and imperial centres.53 Likewise, the subordinate position of the dependent countries can also be explained by the fact that the imperialist powers themselves have actively encouraged capital investment in the dependent countries in accordance with their own interests and needs. The productive structure of the dependent countries, their peculiar relations of production and their participation in the international division of labour have been largely defined by the needs of the capitals based in the imperialist countries and are organised according to these needs.

Historically, unequal exchange has been related to the production of certain commodities for export by capitals located in dependent countries (especially raw materials and food). However, it should be borne in mind that it is in the uneven material and social conditions of production (differences in the productivity of labour, in the composition of capital, etc.) that the basis of unequal exchange is to be found, not in the use-value of commodities.

As a condition of possibility for mutually complementary uneven development, transfers of surplus-value in international trade reproduce inequalities and the specific material conditions under which accumulation of capital on a world scale unfolds. International trade has a key role in the

---

53 "The cheapness of the articles produced by machinery and the revolution in the means of transport and communication provide the weapons for the conquest of foreign markets. By ruining handicraft production of finished articles in other countries, machinery forcibly converts them into fields for the production of its raw material" (Marx, 1992: 579). For his part, Ernest Mandel (1998: 365) considered that "it was the specific structure of the capitalist economy, especially in the age of imperialism but also partly prior to it, which ensured that the accumulation of industrial capital in the metropolitan countries put a decisive brake on the accumulation of industrial capital in the so-called Third World".

development of capitalism, since in addition to redistributing surplus-value it tends to reproduce: the particular forms in which nations trade, the conditions—objective and subjective—necessary for the production of certain kind of use-values, determined and differentiated forms of exploitation of workers, specific historical configurations of the international division of labour, etc. Unequal exchange renders inevitable a polarised development of capitalism on a world scale, thus constituting a core mechanism in the reproduction of what André Gunder Frank (1966) called "the development of underdevelopment".

The basis of unequal exchange lies in the sphere of production: its determinants are the different degree of development of the productive forces in the capitalist world system and the consequently different compositions of capital. Complementarily, these transfers or redistribution of surplus-value take place in the sphere of circulation. This process shows that capitalist reproduction is a complex and contradictory unit of production and circulation.

An example—based on the scheme used by Marx (1993a: 256) in chapter 9 of volume three of *Capital*, although simplified—may be useful to illustrate this.

Scheme 1. Different value-composition of capital, same rate of surplus-value.

Spheres of production	Countries	c	v	Capital invested	Used up c	Surplus-value	Rate of surplus-value	Value of commodities	Cost price	Profit	Price of production	Rate of profit
α	A	60	40	100	51	40	100 %	131	91	22.5	113.5	22.5 %
β	B	95	5	100	10	5	100 %	20	15	22.5	37.5	22.5 %
	Σ	155	45	200	61	45		151	106	45	151	

To simplify the exposition, this chapter assumes that the spheres of production with high composition of capital are located in the imperialist countries and that the spheres with low composition of capital are in the dependent countries. However, the point to be demonstrated is not essentially modified if, instead of assuming that the *whole* sphere is concentrated in a single country, it is posited that the majority of spheres with high composition of capital and of capitals whose composition is above the average of their sphere are persistently located in imperialist countries and that most of the spheres with low composition of capital and of capitals whose composition is below the average of their sphere are located in dependent countries. In any of these cases, the imperialist countries will appropriate surplus-value, since transfers will take place between spheres and capitals within a sphere whose composition is above the average will obtain surplus profits.

As has been explained, if the branches of production or nations were to realise as profit the surplus-value exploited within them, the rates of profit would be substantially different, since the average composition of capital of branches or nations is diverse. Competition in the world market tends to equalise the rates of profit according to the magnitude of capital invested in each branch, in such a way that a general rate of profit tends to be formed in international trade. When this happens, the spheres of production with low composition of capital, located mainly in the dependent countries, systematically transfer surplus-value to the spheres with high composition of capital, located in the imperialist countries, which realise it as profit.

Just as within a country, in the world market the formation of the general rate of profit is a mechanism of *redistribution* of the socially produced surplus-value under the modified form of profit. In this respect, it is important to note that surplus-value is *redistributed* and *transferred* through competition in international trade, but competition does not produce value or surplus-value.

Unequal exchange has its basis in the unevenness in the development of the productive forces (which is expressed as the inequality of compositions of capital) between capitals and spheres of production in the world market. Unequal exchange and dependency appear as relations between nations due to the international division of labour and to the existence of long-term technological and productivity differentials between the capitals, spheres and nations that make up the capitalist world system. States play a crucial role in reinforcing this heterogeneity of the world system by serving as the lever and support of the conditions of reproduction of "their" capitals.

After having set out the tendency towards the formation of an average rate of profit in international trade from the keys given by Marx, let us consider other arguments whereby Marx refers—although not under this denomination—to the transfers of surplus-value in international trade. In the chapter on the counteracting factors to the tendential fall in the rate of profit in volume three of *Capital*, Marx pointed out that

> Capital invested in foreign trade can yield a higher rate of profit ... because it competes with commodities produced by other countries with less developed production facilities, so that the more advanced country sells its goods above their value, even though still more cheaply than its competitors. ... The privileged country receives more labour in exchange for less, even though this difference, the excess, is pocketed by a particular class, just as in the exchange between labour and capital in general. (Marx, 1993a: 344-346)

Commodities produced in "the more advanced country" have a lower individual value and a lower cost price than those produced in the country with "less developed production facilities". For this reason, those commodities can be sold at their international price of production—which is higher than the prevailing price of production within their national borders—and thus yield a higher rate of profit than they would have if the goods were sold within their national borders. This is the mechanism through which the capitals and spheres of production in the dependent countries transfer surplus-value systematically and by which the capitals and branches in imperialist countries permanently realise magnitudes of surplus-value superior to those they exploited. This appropriation of surplus-value through unequal exchange is a counter-tendency to the fall in the rate of profit in the imperialist countries and it may eventually contribute to postpone crises.[54]

Unable to stop the persistent drain of surplus-value in international trade, the capitals located in dependent countries will seek to counter it through a greater and multiform exploitation of the workers in those countries. This issue was raised and developed by Latin American Marxist Ruy Mauro Marini throughout much of his work. When the different forms in which the production of surplus-value is increased lead to the reduction of wages below the value of labour-power, this constitutes a super-exploitation of labour-power (Marini, 2022: 161).

To conclude with the systematisation of the keys provided by Marx to formulate a theoretical approach to the transfers of surplus-value in international trade, let us consider an issue that—as will be seen later, when presenting the contributions of the authors who discussed unequal exchange in the 1960s and 1970s—is relevant for understanding those transfers: national differences in wages. Marx developed this theme in chapter 22 of volume one of *Capital*. However, Marx did not establish there the relationship between the national differences in wages and the formation of prices of production in international trade, since the treatment of the differences between values and prices was still far from being addressed in the logical structure of *Capital* and, as mentioned above, the analysis of the world market was beyond the scope of Marx's *magnum opus*.

In his study on the international differences in wages, Marx pointed out that, first, just as within a nation the magnitude of wages changes over time—with the manifold combinations in the absolute and relative magnitude of wages—there are also simultaneous differences in national wage-levels. Second, he argued that

> In comparing wages in different nations, we must therefore take into account all the factors that determine changes in the amount of the value of labour-power; the price and the extent of the prime necessities of life in their natural and historical development, the cost of training the workers, the part played by the labour of women and

---

54   Like the other counteracting factors to the tendential fall in the rate of profit, international trade only temporarily alleviates the fall but ultimately confirms it and accentuates it.

children, the productivity of labour, and its extensive and intensive magnitude. (Marx, 1992: 701)

Since the treatment of all the factors that determine national differences in wages is beyond the scope of this text, we focus on the productivity of labour and the extent of workers' necessities—both physiological and historically developed.

The extent of the necessities and the way they are satisfied vary from one nation to another not only because of cultural factors, but also—and above all—because the conditions of production and the degree of productivity of labour are different between them.55 The system of human necessities is open and constantly evolving; for Marx, the main factor driving its development is the rise in the productive powers acquired by labour.56 Thus, the rising productivity of labour generates conditions that make it possible to expand the volume of human necessities and to change the way these are satisfied. Therefore, in general, in a nation where the productivity of labour is higher, the system of necessities will tend to be broader and the way necessities are satisfied will potentially be richer and more diverse.57

---

55 "The productivity of labour ... is determined by a wide range of circumstances; it is determined amongst other things by the workers' average degree of skill, the level of development of science and its technological application, the social organization of the process of production, the extent and effectiveness of the means of production, and the conditions found in the natural environment" (Marx, 1992: 130).

56 "At the dawn of civilization, the productive powers acquired by labour are small, but so too are the needs which develop with and upon the means of their satisfaction" (Marx, 1992: 647).

57 "Production thus not only creates an object for the subject, but also a subject for the object. Thus production produces consumption (1) by creating the material for it; (2) by determining the manner of consumption; and (3) by creating the products, initially posited by it as objects, in the form of a need felt by the consumer" (Marx, 1993b: 92). Although the system of necessities develops together with the productive powers acquired by labour ("the means of their satisfaction", as Marx said), it would be wrong to consider, in the case of the capitalist mode of production, that wages tend to increase automatically or proportionally with the productivity of labour. If the system of human necessities and workers' consumption expand under capitalism, it is because within the logic of valorisation that rules this mode of production it is necessary to extend the workers' consumption to realise on an ever-increasing mass of surplus-value. Moreover, it would be equally wrong to consider that under the capitalist mode of production the

In sum, the greater or lesser degree of development of the productivity of labour in one nation relative to another makes it possible for the volume of necessities to be greater or lesser and the magnitude of wages between nations to vary significantly.

Similarly, in dealing with national differences in wages, the distinction between absolute and relative wages is crucial. The absolute wage refers to the price paid by the capitalist for labour-power, while the relative wage refers to the wage compared with surplus-value. Marx pointed out that "it will frequently be found that the daily or weekly wage in the first nation ['the nation with a more developed capitalist mode of production'] is higher than in the second ['the nation with a less developed capitalism'] while the relative price of labour[-power], *i.e.* the price of labour as compared both with surplus-value and with the value of the product, stands higher in the second than in the first" (Marx, 1992: 702).

For Marx, the disparity in wages—both absolute and relative—between nations depends essentially on the difference in the *degree of capitalist development* between them. Therefore, in nations with less-developed productive forces, absolute wages tend to be lower, while relative wages tend to be higher: although in dependent countries the quantity of the means of subsistence necessary to reproduce labour-power is lower, the labour time necessary to produce those means of subsistence is greater because the productive power acquired by labour is less developed there. Thus, in nations with less-developed productive forces, the proportion of the working day in which the labourers produce the equivalent of their wage tends to be greater, while the proportion of the working day during which they deploy surplus labour for the capitalist tends to be smaller. The opposite can be said about imperialist countries: there, the absolute wage tends to be higher, while the relative wage is lower because the rate of surplus-value is higher.

---

development of the productivity of labour automatically implies a qualitative improvement in the way human needs are satisfied. What happens is just the opposite: a progressive deterioration of use-values, the production of degraded use-values, and so on.

But why are national differences in wages relevant to unequal exchange? First, because different wage levels imply *different degrees of exploitation* of labour-power between countries. Second, because the payment of different wages between nations modifies the investment in variable capital made by capitalists in different countries and gives rise to differences in the value-composition of capital. National differences in wages therefore impact the formation of the price of production and the general rate of profit in international trade. Thus, they are one of the main determinations of unequal exchange. This situation was scarcely considered by most Marxists in the first half of the 20th century; even now, its implications are little studied.

Thus, unequal exchange is determined by inequality in the development of productive forces—which translates into different degrees of productivity of labour and different compositions of capital—and national differences in wages—which implies different rates of exploitation between countries and differences in the mass of surplus-value produced, in addition to causing inequalities in the value-composition of capitals. However, even though in analytical terms it is important to distinguish both determinations, it should be noted that inequality in the development of productive forces is preeminent, since—as mentioned above, following Marx's argument—the main determination of national differences in wages is the degree of development of the productive powers acquired by labour in different national spaces.

Unequal exchange contributes to the reproduction of unevenness in the world system and is one of the essential determinations of dependency and underdevelopment. In imperialist countries, the appropriation of surplus-value through international trade fulfils a vital function: it contributes to increase the profitability of capital and to countering the tendency to the fall in the rate of profit. On the other hand, in countries where capitals and branches of production with less developed productive forces are concentrated, the loss of surplus-value has a negative impact on the possibilities for the accumulation of capital and engenders a peculiar form of capitalist reproduction called dependent capitalism. Taken as a whole, these transfers of surplus-value reproduce the inequalities inherent to capitalism as a world system and lead to qualitatively different forms of capital accumulation.

Unequal exchange as seen by the theorists of imperialism

In the first decades of the 20th century, the domination of some nations over others was a recurrent topic within Marxist thought in the context of the debates on imperialism, with authors such as Rosa Luxemburg, Lenin and Bukharin. However, the discussion on the economic function of international trade and the causes of unequal exchange was not central to that debate. In this respect, Henryk Grossman—one of the most important authors of the critique of political economy in the 20th century—considered that

> The problem of the deviation of prices from values in *international* exchange has not been discussed in any systematic way in the Marxist literature, still less integrated into the overall structure of Marx's system, either by Hilferding or anyone else ... So closer analysis of the function of foreign trade under capitalism, from the standpoint of Marx's system, was neglected. (Grossman, 2022: 369)[58]

Therefore, in order to identify the main contributions to the discussion, but also to account for the limited treatment of the subject, a brief account is given below of the main arguments of some authors who contributed to the formulation of the theory of imperialism.

In 1916, Lenin published *Imperialism. The Highest Stage of Capitalism*. The fundamental purpose of that book was "to present ... a general picture of capitalist world economy in its international interrelations" (Lenin, 1937: 9). In *Imperialism...*, Lenin made numerous references to "dependence" and "dependent countries"—which he defined as countries

---

[58] A few pages earlier, Grossman noted: "Bourgeois economics has nothing to say about the true economic function of foreign trade under capitalism. ... The state of understanding the function of foreign trade in the existing Marxist literature is no less dismal" (Grossman, 2022: 359). Likewise, Christian Palloix considered that unequal exchange had been "a practically unapproachable question until now in Marxist theoretical production" (Palloix, 1981: 97).

"which formally are politically independent, but which are in fact en-meshed in the net of financial, and diplomatic dependence"—and used cat-egories such as "uneven development" to account for the tendencies of the capitalist world economy. For example, Lenin (1937: 108) pointed out that "under capitalism there cannot be an *equal* development of different un-dertakings, trusts, branches of industry or countries". The Bolshevik leader also referred to the "super-profits" that imperialist countries obtained through the export of capital to dependent countries. However, although Lenin described some historical forms of domination over the dependent countries (the export of capital and the construction of railroads, among others) and reflected on the uneven development of the capitalist world economy, he did not systematically formulate a conceptual framework to address the dynamics of international trade, nor did he build a theoretical explanation of the mechanisms through which dependency unfolds.

For his part, Nikolai Bukharin addressed the international relations of domination in his work *The World Economy and Imperialism*, published in 1917. Taking as a starting point "a peculiar distribution of the produc-tive forces of world capitalism" (Bukharin, 1972: 22), he formulated rele-vant arguments about aspects of the world economy, such as the interna-tional division of labour, international exchange, the formation of world prices and the specifically social character of world labour.

In his study on the world economy, Bukharin (1972: 27) argued that under imperialism "the whole process of world economic life in modern times reduces itself to the production of surplus value and its distribution among the various groups and sub-groups of ... the world bourgeoisie". For this author, the distribution of surplus-value in the world economy occurs through "the movement of capital", which "is regulated by the law of international equalisation of the rates of profit" (1972: 40). Thus, "in the same way as the international movement of commodities brings the local and 'national' prices to the one and only level of world prices ... so the movement of capital tends to bring the 'national' rates of profit to one level, which tendency expresses nothing but one of the most general laws of the capitalist mode of production on a world scale" (1972: 46). Bukharin also alluded to the "the formation of super-profit under the conditions of

commodity exchange between countries having different economic structures" (1972: 82): he considered that "super-profit has its source in the difference between the social value of the goods (understanding under 'society' world capitalism as a united whole) and their individual value (understanding under 'individual' the 'national economy')" (1972: 84).

Bukharin identified the inequality in the economic structures between countries and the equalisation of the rates of profit in the world market as determining the additional profits appropriated by the imperialist
countries. Despite the significant advances in his formulations on international trade, there are some arguments in his treatment of the subject that
are imprecise or misguided. In spite of the centrality of the uneven development of productive forces in the world economy in Bukharin's starting
point, when speaking about the causes of the international equalisation of
the rate of profit, his explanation focuses on the sphere of circulation and
is not precise enough to emphasise that the basis of such equalisation is the
diversity of the conditions of production: the different compositions of
capital, the different degrees of productivity of labour, etc. An additional
difficulty lies in the unit of analysis chosen by Bukharin: for him, the international equalisation of the rates of profit and the formation of surplus
profits are determined on a national basis. Yet, closely following Marx's
arguments, the average rate of profit and surplus profit in international
trade are formed through competition between capitals and branches of
production with different degrees of development of productive forces in
the world sphere. Lastly, Bukharin (1972: 40) considered that there was a
"law of equalisation of the wage rate" as a result of the international movement of labour-power. This alleged tendency did not exist at the beginning
of the 20th century nor in the 21st century, since the inequalities in the material and social conditions of production between the different national
spaces of value—which is the scale on which the value of labour-power is
determined—have reproduced over time.

It should be noted that throughout the debate on foreign trade some
authors (such as Bukharin or Otto Bauer) confused some particular forms
of production leading to unequal exchange with their general determinations. For example, they considered that transfers of surplus-value took

place between countries producing raw materials and countries producing manufactures. However, as Ernest Mandel (1998: 368) pointed out, "ultimately ... the transfer of value is not tied to a particular type of material production, nor to a particular degree of industrialization, but to a difference in the respective levels of capital accumulation, labour productivity and the rate of surplus-value". Hence, unequal exchange persists even when in the dependent countries the industrialisation processes have some relative advance, since their industrialisation is generally simpler, with lower composition of capital and lower productivity than that prevailing in the imperialist countries, besides depending on the import of means of production from imperialist countries in order to advance.

Among the classical theorists of imperialism, Rosa Luxemburg had a substantially different interpretation of the importance of foreign trade for capitalism. For her, the fundamental economic function of the external market—defined by her, in terms of social economy, as "the non-capitalist social environment which absorbs the products of capitalism and supplies producer goods and labour power for capitalist production"—consisted in serving as a space for the realisation of surplus-value. According to Luxemburg, the capitalist mode of production is not capable of realising the surplus-value produced within itself. She considered that "capitalism needs non-capitalist social organisations as the setting for its development" in order to sell the commodities produced in the capitalist sphere and to realise the surplus-value contained in them. Hence, according to the author of *The Accumulation of Capital*, capitalism can only ensure its own existence as long as it has this non-capitalist environment at its disposal (Luxemburg, 2003: 346-7).

The problem of unequal exchange was addressed with great detail by Henryk Grossman, who researched it theoretically in his work *The Law of Accumulation and Breakdown of the Capitalist System*, published in 1929. It contains one of the clearest explanations of this phenomenon, and is therefore worth quoting extensively. Grossman pointed out that

> As, however, equivalents are not exchanged in international trade, because here too, as on the domestic market, there is a tendency for rates of profit to equalise, it follows that the commodities of the advanced capitalist country, that is a country with a

higher organic composition of capital, are always sold at prices of production higher than their values; while, conversely, with free competition the commodities of countries with a lower organic composition of capital are sold at prices of production that must, as a rule, be lower than their values. ... In this way *transfers* of surplus value occur on the world market, and *within the sphere of circulation*, from undeveloped to more developed capitalist countries.

... The same principle applies to price formation on the world market as governs prices in a conceptually *isolated* capitalism. But the latter is simply an auxiliary theoretical construction and only the *world market* as the unity of different national economies is a real and concrete phenomenon .... Just as *within* a conceptually isolated capitalism entrepreneurs equipped with technologies more advanced than the social average make *an extra profit* at the expense of those entrepreneurs whose techniques remain behind the social average, when they sell their commodities at socially average prices, so *on the world market the most technologically developed countries obtain super profits at the expense of countries whose technological and economic development is backward*. Marx points out that this function of foreign trade has been a constant feature of the capitalist mode of production since' it began (Grossman, 2022: 371-372).

... the gain of the more advanced capitalist country signifies a *transfer* of profit from the less developed country ... there arises for the more developed country, alongside the surplus value produced in the country itself, an *additional* surplus value which is produced in the less developed country and *transferred* to the more developed country by means of competition on the world market, that is an *unequal exchange*, an exchange of non-equivalents. This transfer of surplus value from one country to another is the result of their different stages of economic development. The same transfer of value occurs in foreign trade with another capitalist country, so long as it is technologically and economically less developed (Grossman, 2022: 374).

... an *injection of surplus value* from the outside by means of foreign trade must raise the rate of profit and thus *moderate and weaken the breakdown tendency* ... According to our conception, which I believe I have demonstrated is also Marx's, in keeping with the law of value, the mass of the original surplus value is *augmented* by means of transfers from abroad. The super profit that flows from the sale of commodities above their values is a gain that is obtained on the margins of a capitalist economy by means of foreign trade. ... At more advanced phases of capital accumulation ... the question of injecting additional profit from outside by way of foreign trade becomes *a matter of life and death for capitalism*. (Grossman, 2022: 374-375)

According to Grossman, the equalisation of the rates of profit and the transfers of surplus-value occur between countries, not between branches of production.59 In fact, in the section devoted to "Foreign trade and the sale of commodities at prices of production deviating from their values" he barely mentions the different branches of production. On the contrary: as argued above, transfers of surplus-value are due to the inequality in the material and social conditions of production between capitals and branches. Although unequal exchange appears as transfers of surplus-value between nations, it is not in that scale that its basis is to be found.

In these passages, Grossman presents the most important elements for the discussion on unequal exchange, which is one of the main processes that determine imperialism and dependency. His main contributions to the debate can be summarised in the following points:

1. Competition in the world market is the main driving force behind the transfers or flows of surplus-value known as unequal exchange.

3. The determination of the transfers of surplus-value in international trade lies in the different degree of development of productive forces between capitals and branches of production competing in the world market, as well as in the consequently different compositions of capital existing between them.

4. In international trade, there is competition between spheres of production with different compositions of capital and rates of profit which are originally very different. Since the same principle that regulates price formation within a country or in a "conceptually isolated capitalism" operates in the world market, in international trade there is a tendency towards the formation of a general rate of profit.

---

59 For example, he pointed out that "this transfer of surplus value from one country to another is the result of their different stages of economic development" (Grossman, 2022: 374).

5.   As a result of this tendency in international trade, countries where the spheres of production with higher technological development and higher composition of capital are located sell their commodities at prices of production which are above their values (*i.e.*, there is a difference between the surplus-value produced and the surplus-value appropriated), thus receiving transfers of surplus-value-from the countries with a lower development of productive forces.

6.   On the other hand, the countries where the branches with less-developed productive forces tend to concentrate and whose composition of capital is lower persistently transfer a part of the value produced there to the imperialist countries.

7.   In this way, through the circulation of commodities and competition in international trade, there is a *redistribution* of socially produced surplus-value. The additional surplus-value appropriated by capitals and branches of production located in the imperialist countries is the result of transfers of surplus-value exploited in the dependent countries, as a result of the inequality in their material and social conditions of production.

8.   The transfers of surplus-value in international trade from dependent to imperialist countries and the surplus profit that the latter appropriate do not constitute a violation of the law of value; on the contrary, they are a result of its validity in the world market.

9.   The injection of surplus-value through foreign trade moderates the tendential fall in the rate of profit in imperialist countries. This becomes increasingly important as capitalism develops and this tendential fall is accentuated.

It should be noted that for Grossman a characteristic of the capitalist mode of production is the persistent tendency towards overproduction and over-accumulation of capital, which leads to insufficient valorisation and crises. In this sense, the most important economic function of foreign trade is that it is the means through which imperialist countries receive an injection of surplus-value which moderates the tendential fall in the rate of profit.

Thus, for Grossman, imperialist expansion is explained by the need to carry out an "increased valorisation" of capital and to raise the mass of appropriated profits through the transfer of surplus-value from abroad. Then, the reason behind imperialist expansion is not the search for a non-capitalist environment which absorbs the products of capitalism and supplies raw materials, as Luxemburg proposed.

The question of the transfers of surplus-value in international trade was practically settled by Grossman. However, even in his detailed treatment of the subject, it was not completely resolved. One crucial point was still missing: the national differences in wages—and, therefore, the different rates of surplus-value in the world system. The task of continuing the discussion was left to later authors, who contributed decisive elements to it.

The French debate on "unequal exchange" in the 1960s and 1970s

For Bukharin and Grossman, the causes of transfers of surplus-value in international trade were the uneven development of the productive forces between nations and the tendency towards the equalisation of the rates of profit in the world market. However, a point that was not explicitly considered by these authors (nor by other Marxists) was that of national differences in wages as a cause of transfers of surplus-value in international trade. As mentioned above, national differences in wages are relevant because they impact investment in variable capital, the different rates of exploitation between nations and, therefore, the formation of the price of production and the general rate of profit in international trade. This important dimension of the problem was extensively dealt with in the 1960s and 1970s by numerous French or French-based authors: Arghiri Emmanuel, Charles Bettelheim, Samir Amin and Christian Palloix, among others.

The author whose intervention gave rise to the French debate on unequal exchange was Arghiri Emmanuel. It is therefore necessary to begin by recovering his arguments. The publication of his *Unequal Exchange* sparked an intense debate on the reasons for the economic inequalities between nations. In that debate, Emmanuel's central theses were firmly rejected by authors such as Charles Bettelheim and Ernest Mandel, not only due to theoretical inconsistencies (mainly considering that the price of production is equal to the sum of the "rewards for the factors" or taking wages as an "independent variable"), but also because of the political implications of his arguments—particularly his shift of the main antagonism of capitalism as a world system from class contradiction to an alleged contradiction between nations.60

In a critical balance, it should be noted that the main merits of Emmanuel's intervention (besides its inconsistencies and the necessary criticisms that were raised against it) were 1) to question Ricardian theses on comparative advantages in international trade, which supposedly lead to a mutually beneficial exchange for the countries that participate in international trade, and 2) to trigger a broad debate on the national differences in wages as one of the causes of unequal exchange—although, as will be seen, his interpretation was inaccurate. In this sense, some of this author's arguments on the dynamics of international trade, as well as their critical reception, are reviewed below.

In his book on the subject, Emmanuel (1972: 265) pointed out that "unequal exchange is only one of the mechanisms whereby value is transferred from one group of countries to another ... I think it is possible to state that unequal exchange is the *elementary* transfer mechanism, and that, as such, it enables the advanced countries to begin and regularly give new impetus to that *unevenness of development*". For this author, although there are other mechanisms for the transfer of surplus-value between countries (such as the payment of interest on external debt or repatriation of profits by multinational enterprises), these are secondary, since the *elementary transfer mechanism* is unequal exchange.

Where does unequal exchange come from? Emmanuel summarises his argument as follows: "we call 'unequal exchange' the price relation

---

60 For a detailed critique of Emmanuel's work, see the comments by Charles Bettelheim (1972).

established by virtue of the law of the levelling of the rate of profit between regions of different ... rates of surplus value" (1981: 20). In this definition, Emmanuel indicates three key elements: 1) unequal exchange is a *price relation* which 2) is established due to the equalisation of the rates of profit 3) between regions with different rates of surplus-value.

Emmanuel's definition explicitly points to an aspect that received little attention in the previous treatment of the subject: unequal exchange occurs between countries with different rates of surplus-value. However, for this author, differences in the rates of surplus-value are not the result of the unevenness of productive forces between nations (and, therefore, of the different levels of productivity), but of international differences in wages.[61] For this author, only those transfers of surplus-value resulting from national differences in wages can properly be considered as "unequal exchange". Let us clarify this point.

Emmanuel considered that world prices were "the starting point of the problem of unequal exchange" (Emmanuel, 1981: 11). The basis of his argument was the tendency towards the formation of a general rate of profit in international trade. While he recognised the importance of the formation of prices of production in international trade, he did not consider that the differences between production and appropriation of surplus-value resulting from the equalisation of rates of profit corresponded to an "unequal exchange" strictly speaking. For this author, the transfers of surplus-value from the country with low composition of capital to the country with a higher composition of capital do not constitute an "unequal exchange": the sale of commodities at their prices of production (not at their values) does not constitute an "inequality" in capitalist terms but, on the contrary, are a result of the equalisation of the rates of profit (see

---

61   In Emmanuel's argument, prices of production are not "subject to determination by the relations of production and the productive forces" (Bettelheim, 1972: 279), but they are the result of the sum of "rewards for the factors". Moreover, he considers wages as an "independent variable".

scheme 2).62 For Emmanuel, if transfers of surplus-value from one sphere or production with low composition of capital to another with high composition of capital within a country are not called "unequal exchange", there is no reason to speak of unequal exchange when there are transfers of surplus-value in international trade resulting from differences in composition of capital.63 Even so, it is important to remember that, due to the inherently unbalanced character of the reproduction of capitalism, "international exchanges, under the formalism of equivalence, reveal a profound inequality" (Palloix, 1981: 98)

---

62   It is relevant to highlight that Emmanuel did not deny the existence of transfers of surplus-value between countries with different compositions of capital. What he rejected is that these transfers should be defined as an "unequal exchange".

63   In this respect, Samir Amin (1981: 78-79) considered that "Emmanuel is right in asserting that, in this case, although the exchange does not ensure the same quantity of products for each hour of total labour, it is not unequal, because 'unequal' exchanges of this kind characterise relations within a nation, since 'prices of production ... constitute an element immanent to the competitive system'". He also pointed out that "Emmanuel rightly describes this exchange [the one based on wage inequality between countries], and only this, as true unequal exchange" (Amin, 1981: 81).

Scheme 2. Different organic compositions of capital, same rate of surplus-value[64]

Spheres of production	Countries	c	v	Capital invested	Used up c	Surplus-value	Rate of surplus-value	Value of commodities	Cost price	Profit	Price of production	Rate of profit
α	A	850	50	900	200	50	100 %	300	250	90	340	10 %
β	B	50	50	100	10	50	100 %	110	60	10	70	10 %
	Σ	900	100	1000	210	100		410	310	100	410	

64 This scheme is based on Emmanuel (1981).

Emmanuel and Amin both argued that companies competing in international trade have similar degrees of technological development, regardless of the branch of production in which they operate and whether they are in imperialist or dependent countries. For these authors, since the technical composition of capital among capitals and spheres of production exporting to the world market is similar, the productivity of labour is tendentially the same between countries. However, since "the value of labour-power ... is not determined by the average international conditions of reproduction, but by the specifically national conditions of reproduction" (Palloix, 1981: 124),65 workers with similar levels of productivity receive very different wages: high wages in imperialist countries, low wages in dependent ones.

Let us consider a situation in which two spheres of production (one located in an imperialist country, the other in a dependent country) have the same *technical* composition of capital and equal levels of productivity and intensity of labour. In both spheres, commodities representing the same magnitude of value will be produced in a working day. However, since wages are lower in the dependent country, the investment in variable capital by the companies operating there is lower, the mass of surplus-value is higher and the rate of surplus-value is higher. As a result, despite having produced commodities that represent the same magnitude of value, these spheres of production would have rates of profit which are originally different due to the national differences in wages. In this case, as the rates of profit equalise between the spheres due to competition in international trade, there will be a transfer of surplus-value from the country with lower wages to the country with higher wages (see scheme 3). According to Emmanuel and Amin, "this type of exchange would be unequal even from the point of view of capitalist production" (Bettelheim, 1981: 35). For this reason, they called it unequal exchange in the strict or narrow sense.

---

65   In this respect, Emmanuel considered that "from the point of view of wages, national borders constitute thresholds of discontinuity" (1981: 17).

Emmanuel's proposal consisted in applying Marx's scheme of the equalisation of the rates of profit by introducing an additional variable, which Marx excluded from his analysis in *Capital*: the different rates of surplus-value between nations resulting from national differences in wages. He argued that the new scheme "in no way expresses a law contrary to Marx's" (Emmanuel, 1981: 19). Let us consider the formation of prices of production when branches located in different countries have the same technical composition of capital but different value-composition and different rates of surplus-value due to the wage differences between countries.

Scheme 3. Same technical composition, different value-composition of capital and different rates of surplus-value

Spheres of production	Countries	c	v	Capital invested	Used up c	Surplus-value	Rate of surplus-value	Value of commodities	Cost price	Profit	Price of production	Rate of profit
α	A	850	50	900	200	50	100 %	300	250	74.36	324.36	8.26 %
β	B	850	5	855	200	95	1900 %	300	205	70.64	275.64	8.26 %
	Σ	1700	55	1755	400	145		600	455	145	600	

In the above scheme, the *technical* composition of capital is the same in the two spheres of production located in the two countries (*i.e.*, the technological conditions of the production process are identical). Since national wages are different, the value-composition of capital of the spheres of production is different even though they have the same technical composition of capital. In these circumstances, the rate and mass of surplus-value produced by each sphere are different. As a result, their rates of profit are originally very different. As in the cases previously considered, the rates of profit of the different branches tend to equalise under the pressure of competition in international trade. However, in this case, the formation of international prices of production takes place on the basis of rates of profit whose original diversity lies in national differences in wages.

Thus, unequal exchange is not only the result of the unevenness in the technical composition of capital, but also of wage differences and variations in the rates of surplus-value between nations. This situation was considered by Marx, who pointed out that differences in the rates of surplus-value were the most important determination of differences in the rate of profit between nations: "We may remark in passing that different national rates of profit generally depend on different national rates of surplus-value" (Marx, 1993a: 250).

A central problem in Emmanuel's formulation is that by considering differences in wages as the only cause of unequal exchange and by treating wages as an independent variable he came to wrong conclusions: "since the deterioration of the terms of trade reflects the difference in the rate of surplus-value, perhaps the underdeveloped countries could, by sharply increasing wages, make the inequality of exchanges disappear" (Emmanuel, 1981: 22). It should be noted that for Emmanuel the level of wages (which imply different rates of surplus-value) is not determined by the degree of development of productive forces or by the prevailing relations of production, but is a "reward" that can be modified arbitrarily and independently of any change in the material and social conditions of production. On the contrary: based on Marx's perspective, the level of wages is not an independent variable that is externally or arbitrarily determined, but a result of the material and social conditions of production, which differ between nations. Productive forces and relations of production are the objective basis on which wages are determined (Bettelheim, 1972; Mandel, 1998).

Even if the arbitrary wage increase proposed by Emmanuel happened, it would not change the inequalities in the development of productive forces between spheres and countries; therefore, such an increase would not put an end to transfers of surplus-value in international trade. As long as there are differences in the degree of development of productive forces between branches of industry and nations, the basis for transfers of surplus-value in international trade and for the reproduction of inequalities in the world system will continue to exist.

Despite Emmanuel's errors (considering prices of production as the sum of the "rewards for the factors", taking wages as an "independent variable", viewing antagonism between nations as the central contradiction of the capitalist world system), his intervention contributed to broadening the discussion on the causes of unequal exchange by explicitly pointing out the importance of national differences in wages.

As seen above, according to Emmanuel the transfers of surplus-value resulting from the different compositions of capital between branches and nations should not be considered unequal exchange in the narrow or strict sense. This one-sided treatment of the problem posed a false dilemma. To explain how inequalities in the world system are reproduced through international trade, it is necessary to account for the fact that the differences in the development of productive forces between branches and capitals settled in different nations, as well as national differences in wages, are determinations of the transfers of surplus-value in international trade.

A synthesis that overcame the false dilemma posed by Emmanuel in this discussion was put forward by Charles Bettelheim. He made a detailed criticism of Emmanuel's arguments and considered that his conclusions were a particular case within the general category of unequal exchange resulting from the different compositions of capital between nations. In Bettelheim's (1981: 34) words, the "unequal exchange ... studied by Emmanuel [due to national differences in wages] constitutes in a certain way a particular category within the general category" of unequal exchange due to differences in the composition of capital.

Bettelheim pointed out an issue that was not considered by Emmanuel due to the unilateral way in which he formulated his argument: the causes of the transfers of surplus-value in international trade do not exist independently, but feed back on each other. Bettelheim put it in the following terms: "Emmanuel's analysis shows that when certain countries have a lower organic composition of capital than the countries with which they exchange and *also have* a lower wage rate (*i.e.*, a higher rate of surplus-value), *the inequality of exchange is further aggravated*" (Bettelheim, 1981: 35).

In sum, the general determination of unequal exchange is the inequality in the level of development of productive forces between capitals, branches and nations in the world market, which is expressed in differences in the composition of capital and in national differences in wages. Moreover, the particular determinations of unequal exchange coexist and feed back on each other.

Christian Palloix, for his part, tried to identify the logical and historical relationship between the determinations of the transfers of surplus-value: "for us, one is not dissociated from the other, since unequal exchange in the narrow sense [due to the national differences in wages] is the result of the evolution of unequal exchange in the broad sense [which results from differences in the level of development of productive forces]" (1981: 116). And he adds that the transfer of surplus-value due to the disparity in the level of productive forces "becomes the basis of inequality [in exchanges] due to the level of wages between nations" (Palloix, 1981: 119). For Palloix, because of the disparity in technological development and productivity between nations, one hour of work in the dependent country will be equivalent to less than one hour of work in the imperialist country. "This process constitutes the first foundation of the undervaluation of the value of labour-power in the [underdeveloped] nation, concurrent to the inequality of wages in the long-term dynamics" (Palloix, 1981: 118-119). According to this author, the only way in which underdeveloped countries can compete in the world market is through the undervaluation of labour-

power, and he considers that "the international price of production conse-
crates this undervaluation" (Palloix, 1981: 123).

Palloix pointed to an issue whose consideration is very important for
thinking about dependency: unequal exchange resulting from the disparity
in the development of productive forces is the foundation of what he called
the "undervaluation" of labour-power in dependent countries. The low
level of development of productive forces creates the conditions for structurally lower wages in dependent countries.

For him, the so-called "undervaluation" of labour-power meant that
in the dependent countries the value of labour-power is lower, but it is fully
paid. From the perspective of Marxist dependency theory, it could be argued, going one step further, that the transfers of surplus-value in international trade resulting from inequality in the development of the productive
forces are the foundation not only of a lower value of labour-power, but
also of *the payment of labour-power below its value* as a way in which capitalists in the dependent countries seek to compensate for such transfers.
The fall in wages contributes to further aggravate the transfers of surplus-
value that originated it. What has been pointed out here about national
differences in wages as a particular determination of unequal exchange
leads to formulating an important conclusion on this issue: *the super-exploitation of labour-power—i.e., the payment of labour-power below its
value—is not only a result but also a determination of transfers of surplus-
value in international trade.*

Schemes 2 and 4 illustrate the above. Scheme 2 shows that, as a result
of the different level of development of productive forces between spheres
α and β—which is manifested in different technical and value compositions of capital—and of the equalisation of the rates of profit with respect
to the capital invested, the sphere of production with the lowest composition of capital, β, located in country B, must sell its commodities at a price
of production which is below their value and thus realises as profit only a
part of the surplus-value which it exploited directly in the production process. As a way of compensating for this unfavourable transfer of surplus-
value and of retaining for themselves a greater magnitude of surplus-value,
the capitals of the less technologically developed branch, settled in the

dependent countries, transfer—to put it in Palloix's terms—this "under-valuation of the product" to the value of labour-power. This leads to the situation represented in the following scheme:

Scheme 4. Different technical and value-composition of capital, different rate of surplus-value

Spheres of production	Countries	c	v	Capital invested	Used up c	Surplus-value	Rate of surplus-value	Value of commodities	Cost price	Profit	Price of production	Rate of profit
α	A	850	50	900	200	50	100 %	300	250	110.20	360.20	12.24 %
β	B	50	30	80	10	70	233 %	110	40	9.80	49.80	12.24 %
	Σ	900	80	980	210	120		410	290	120	410	

The reduction in wages in branch β and in country B leads to a lower investment in variable capital and to a higher rate of surplus-value in the dependent country. This reduction in wages also implies that when the rates of profit equalise in international trade, a price of production is formed in which surplus-value is transferred not only because of the disparity in the level of development of productive forces but also because of the international differences in wages and rates of surplus-value. In this case, the rate of profit increases for both countries. In this way, the capitalists of the branches located in the imperialist countries benefit from the decrease in wages in the dependent countries, as the valorisation of their capital increases.

To sum up: the payment of low wages—which can be the payment of wages below the value of labour-power—in the dependent countries serves as a compensation mechanism for the transfer of surplus-value to the spheres located in the imperialist countries. Since it translates into a higher rate of surplus-value, the payment of lower wages allows capitalists in the dependent countries to partially counterbalance the drain of surplus-value and to obtain a higher rate of profit. However, it does nothing to change the conditions that make the transfers of surplus-value possible, and it even aggravates and accentuates them. This generates a deeply pernicious dynamic for dependent countries: the causes that lead to unequal exchange coexist, intertwine and feed back, and the workers of the these countries are exploited on an ever greater scale.

Unequal exchange (due to differences in the composition of capital, differences in wages or the conjunction of both) is a means through which inequalities in the world system are reproduced, since the spheres of production and capitals of the imperialist countries appropriate more value than they produced and valorise a part of the surplus-value that was produced by workers in the dependent countries. In these circumstances, the conditions for accumulation of capitals and spheres of production in imperialist nations are enhanced by an injection of surplus-value from outside. The systematic transfer of surplus-value from the spheres and capitals in the dependent countries to the imperialist ones limits the conditions for accumulation of the former, while it makes possible the accumulation of additional surplus-value and attenuates the fall of the rate of profit in the latter. In sum, unequal exchange contributes to the reproduction on an expanded scale of underdevelopment and dependency.

Two relevant interventions from Trotskyism: Ernest Mandel and Roman Rosdolsky

Contemporaneous to this debate on unequal exchange, two Trotskyist intellectuals, Ernest Mandel and Roman Rosdolsky, formulated important reflections on the economic function of foreign trade. Both authors agreed that unequal exchange is relevant to explain the uneven development of capitalism as a world system and recognised the role of foreign trade as a means of expropriating and transferring value from underdeveloped countries to imperialist ones. Unlike the French-based authors, who focused their interpretation of unequal exchange on international variations in wages and the resulting differences in rates of surplus-value, Mandel and Rosdolsky emphasised the importance of differences in productivity between countries as a determination of unequal exchange.

Let us begin with Ernest Mandel's arguments. For this author, the reason for unequal exchange—which he understood as "the exchange of *unequal* quantities of labour" (Mandel, 1998: 351)—"comes down in the last analysis to the difference in the level of productivity (socially necessary expenditure of labour) between the two types of country" (Mandel, 1968: 477), namely imperialist and underdeveloped. Therefore, "unequal exchange on the world market ... is always the result of a difference in the average productivity of labour between two nations" (Mandel, 1998: 66). Mandel based his interpretation of unequal exchange on a passage from chapter 22 of volume one of *Capital*, "National Differences in Wages", in which Marx pointed out that

> the law of value is yet more modified in its international application by the fact that, on the world market, national labour which is more productive also counts as more

intensive, as long as the more productive nation is not compelled by competition to lower the selling price of its commodities to the level of their value.

... The different quantities of commodities of the same kind, produced in different countries in the same working time, have, therefore, unequal international values, which are expressed in different prices. (Marx, 1992: 702)

Thus, for Mandel, since the most productive national labour process *counts as* more intensive, in international trade, the country with higher productivity sells the product of one hour of labour and receives in return the product of more labour time—say, two hours—from the country with lower productivity. This is what Mandel meant when he pointed out that

Equal international values are exchanged for equal international values. Where then, does the 'unequal exchange' lie hidden behind this equivalence? It is to be found in the fact that these equal international values represent *unequal quantities of labour*. (Mandel, 1998: 359)

It is important to note that in this passage Mandel argues that in international trade commodities are exchanged according to their "equal international values"—which represent unequal quantities of labour time—and not according to their prices of production. This is because, as will be seen below, he states that there is no tendency in international trade to the equalisation of the rates of profit.

Where does the additional value appropriated by imperialist countries through international trade come from? In this respect, Mandel considered that the surplus-profits appropriated by capitals, spheres of production and countries with higher productivity are the result of a redistribution or transfer of surplus-value from capitals, spheres and countries operating under conditions of lower productivity. Thus, the additional value appropriated by capitals located in imperialist countries has its origin in the labour deployed in underdeveloped ones. For Mandel, transfers of surplus-value are the result of international productivity differentials. These transfers make it possible to understand why in the whole capitalist system

development and underdevelopment reciprocally determine each other ... surplus-profit can only be achieved at the expense of less productive countries, regions and branches of production. Hence development takes place only in juxtaposition with underdevelopment; it perpetuates the latter and itself develops thanks to this perpetuation.

Without underdeveloped regions, there can be no transfer of surplus to the industrialized regions and hence no acceleration of capital accumulation there. (Mandel, 1998: 102)

Mandel acknowledged that unequal exchange is a relevant process in the relationship between development and underdevelopment in the capitalist world market. However, something peculiar in his argument, which distinguishes it from that of other authors on this subject, is that he considered that in international trade there is no tendency towards the equalisation of the rates of profit. He argued that "the hypothesis of international equalization of the rates of profit cannot be sustained—either theoretically or empirically. Theoretically, it presupposes perfect international mobility of capital" (Mandel, 1998: 352). The Belgian Trotskyist pointed out that in order for there to be a tendency towards the formation of a general rate of profit in international trade "there would have to be unrestricted free international movement of capital and this simply does not exist" (Mandel, 1998: 352).

In relation to Mandel's denial of the equalisation of the rates of profit in international trade, it should be pointed out that for the tendency towards the formation of a general rate of profit to operate, it is not necessary for there to be "free" and "unrestricted" movement of capital, nor for there to be "perfect" competition. If these were the conditions for the formation of the average rate of profit, it would not even operate within national borders. On the contrary, as Mariano Féliz argues:

the unrestricted mobility of capital in the neoclassical sense (without restrictions, with an indefinitely large number of small capitals) does not define the possibility of configuring international prices of production and the process of equalisation of the rate of profit. On the contrary, this results from the existence of a process of real competition that does occur on a global scale between large capitals. (Féliz, 2021: 122)

Therefore, for the tendency towards the formation of a general rate of profit in international trade to operate, having real capitalist competition and movement of capital suffices. This tendency will be more pronounced the more intense this competition and movement are.

Throughout his work, Mandel insisted that a characteristic of imperialism and late capitalism was the increasing importance of the international mobility of capital. Despite this, he denied that in international trade commodities were sold at their international price of production. Mandel's refusal to consider that in international trade there is an equalisation of the rates of profit stemmed from the fact that, in his understanding, this would imply "the equalization of all economic, social and political conditions" of capitalism on a world scale.66 "Such equalization", Mandel argued, "is completely contradicted by the law of uneven and combined development which dominates this development" (1998: 352).

Now, would the formation of an average rate of profit in international trade entail, in effect, the homogenisation of national rates of profit towards a single world rate of profit and lead to the levelling of all economic, social and political conditions of capitalism on a world scale? No. First, because the tendency towards the formation of an average rate of profit in international trade does not imply that there are no longer differences in national rates of profit. In capitalism, multiple national spheres of commodity circulation coexist simultaneously with an international sphere of commodity circulation. These are two complementary and contradictory scales—national and global—of the deployment of capital. The "formation of uniform prices of production on a world-wide scale" invoked by Mandel would only happen if there were no national borders, differentiated state policies, etc., which relatively limit competition and the mobility of capital. Since these barriers exist and form differentiated national spheres of commodity circulation, the rates of profit are different between nations. In turn, these national rates of profit differ from the average rate of profit in the international sphere of commodity circulation.

---

66 In his critique of those who argued that there was a tendency towards the formation of international prices of production, Mandel acknowledged that the international mobility of capital would have as its "logical corollary" the "formation of uniform prices of production on a world-wide scale" (1998: 352).

Only capitals and branches of industry competing in international trade participate in the formation of the average rate of profit in international trade.

Second, the formation of an average rate of profit in international trade does not lead to the elimination of unevenness of development in capitalism because it implies the *redistribution* of surplus-value from capitals, branches of industry and countries with a lower level of development of the productive forces to those with a higher one. As a result of this redistribution of surplus-value, capitals, branches and countries with higher composition of capital have an increased valorisation due to an injection of surplus-value from abroad, while those with lower composition of capital have a decreased valorisation. Consequently, transfers of surplus-value in international trade reduce the rate of accumulation of productive capital within dependent countries and—as Marxist dependency theory has emphatically argued—give rise to differentiated forms of capital reproduction, which in turn tend to reproduce national unevenness and heterogeneities of development.

Ernest Mandel did not incorporate the formation of prices of production in international trade into his analysis, as he limited his treatment of unequal exchange to the determination of the international value of commodities in foreign trade, taking into account differences in productivity and labour intensity between countries. As argued in the preceding sections, it is necessary to make a more concrete analysis and consider the formation of the general rate of profit in international trade.

Although it is difficult to empirically show the tendency towards the formation of a general rate of profit in international trade, recently some authors such as Guglielmo Carchedi and Michael Roberts (2021) have conducted relevant research in that area. Their findings—which require further research to support them—offer suggestive indications about the tendency towards the equalisation of the rates of profit in international trade and about the magnitude of unequal exchange.

To conclude with the recovery of Ernest Mandel's arguments on this subject, it is important to point out that the productivity differentials that this author considered to be the cause of unequal exchange have their material basis in the different levels of development of productive forces. In other words, productivity differentials are fundamentally a result of the uneven development of productive forces between capitals, branches of industry and countries. Therefore, what Mandel considered as the main cause of unequal exchange—*i.e.*, differences in productivity—is in fact a particular determination of it, which is explained by its general determination: inequality in the development of productive forces and the corresponding social conditions of production.

Ukrainian Marxist Roman Rosdolsky also considered differences in labour intensity and productivity between countries as determinations of unequal exchange. Rosdolsky based his interpretation of this process on the aforementioned passage from chapter 22 of volume one of *Capital*, in which Marx argued that the more productive national working day counts as more intense, as well as on a passage from *Theories of Surplus-Value*, in which, discussing the "disintegration of the Ricardian school", Marx pointed out that in

> trade between different countries... even according to Ricardo's theory, three days of labour of one country can be exchanged against one of another country ... Here the law of value undergoes essential modification. The relationship between labour days of different countries may be similar to that existing between skilled, complex labour, and unskilled, simple labour within a country. In this case, the richer country exploits the poorer one, even where the latter gains by the exchange. (Marx, 1971: 105-106)

In *The Making of Marx's 'Capital'*, Rosdolsky pointed out that unlike colonial appropriation, whose basis is political and military domination over colonised territories, unequal exchange between formally independent nations is a form of appropriation "which in no way makes use of means of political domination, which is not intentional, but which simply comes about by virtue of the economic laws operating in capitalism" (Rosdolsky, 1977: 309). For Rosdolsky, unequal exchange results from the modified form of the operation of the law of value in the world market:

> Within one country the differences in intensity and productivity of labour become equalised at one socially average level. But this does not apply on the world market!

'The more intense national labour, as compared with the less intense' not only produces 'in the same time more value, which expresses itself in more money'; here, the
law of value 'is yet more modified ... by the fact that on the world market, national
labour which is more productive also counts as more intensive...' The result is that
an unequal exchange takes place between different nations .... 'In this case, the richer
country exploits the poorer one (even where the latter gains by the exchange)' ...
'just as a manufacturer who employs a new invention before it becomes generally
used ... valorises the specifically higher productivity of the labour he employs as
surplus labour', and therefore achieves a surplus profit. Except in this situation the
surplus profit is not temporary, as with the case of the individual manufacturer, but
permanent in its nature. ... It is not necessary to point out what this unequal exchange means in terms of losses for the poorer country, which thus continually has
to give away a portion of its national labour. (Rosdolsky, 1977: 310)

In addition to considering productivity and intensity differentials,
Rosdolsky incorporated the equalisation of the rates of profit into his explanation of unequal exchange. He pointed out that

In addition to this, Henryk Grossmann believed he could put forward another reason why the backward nations are exploited by the advanced capitalist countries in
international trade; namely the inequality in the composition of their capitals. Insofar as a tendency to equalisation of the rate of profit exists in international trade, 'the
commodities of the capitalistically highly developed country, *i.e.* a country with a
higher than average composition of capital, will be sold at prices of production which
are always higher than their values; whereas inversely, in the countries with a lower
organic composition of capital, commodities, under free competition, will be sold at
prices of production which as a rule must be lower than their value ... In this way
transfers of the surplus-value produced in the underdeveloped country to the capitalistically higher developed will take place on the world market within the sphere of
circulation'. (Rosdolsky, 1977: 310-311)

Analogous to what was noted above about Ernest Mandel, Rosdolsky's argument about productivity differentials as a determination of unequal exchange is correct, but it is a result of the *fundamental determination* to
which Henryk Grossmann referred, and which Rosdolsky seems to consider secondary: *the different level of development of the productive forces*,
which is expressed in the inequality of compositions of capital and which
results in different levels of productivity of labour between capitals,
branches of industry and nations. What Rosdolsky considers a particular

case ("another reason") is in fact the general case, the fundamental deter-mination.

It is worth highlighting some elements in the argument put forward by Rosdolsky. First, that unequal exchange is not an intentional process through which the imperialist powers plunder the dominated countries. On the contrary: unequal exchange is a spontaneous, unintended result of the operation of the law of value in the world market. Second, that the "sur-plus-profit" appropriated by the highly developed capitalist nations (those with high productivity and high composition of capital) results from the "exploitation" of underdeveloped countries (with low productivity and low composition of capital). Lastly, that the surplus-profit appropriated in in-ternational trade by the capitals and branches located in the highly devel-oped capitalist countries are not temporary, as in the case of the individual producer who momentarily operates in the best productive conditions but are "permanent in their nature" due to the international division of labour.

Regarding the passages from Marx's work cited by Mandel and Rosdolsky to support their interpretation of unequal exchange on the basis of productivity differentials, it is interesting to note that in these excerpts Marx drew unclear analogies between the most productive national labour, the most intensive labour and complex or skilled labour for the study of international trade. These three concepts—productivity, intensity and complexity—are clearly different in the Marxian argument and have dif-ferent implications for the determination of the magnitude of value of commodities. More intensive labour and complex labour are represented in a higher magnitude of value of commodities. Conversely, although more productive labour produces more use-values, it is represented in a lower magnitude of value per individual commodity, since higher productivity implies less expenditure of human labour-power to produce each unit of use-value.

The interpretation proposed here argues that the additional surplus-value appropriated by capitals, spheres of production and countries with a higher development of the productive forces and therefore with a higher composition of capital is not the representation of the more productive la-bour employed by them, since more productive labour is represented in a lower magnitude of value of the individual commodity, not in a higher magnitude of value. On the contrary, this additional surplus-value, this increased valorisation, is the result of a *redistribution* or *transfer* of value from those capitals, spheres of production and nations with a lower composition of capital.67 That is why development and imperialism cannot be explained without underdevelopment and dependency.

Lastly, it is relevant to note that although Ernest Mandel and Roman Rosdolsky emphatically denied that capitalism permanently tended towards the absolute pauperisation of the working class, they considered that in the so-called underdeveloped countries there were objective tendencies which led to wages being persistently below the value of labour-power. In this respect, Mandel (1998: 67-68) pointed out that in underdeveloped countries "the commodity of labour-power is in its turn not only sold at its declining value, but even *below* this value" due to the prevalence of an enormous industrial reserve army. For his part, Rosdolsky considered that "tendencies towards immiseration" were permanently operating "in the so-called underdeveloped areas of the world" (1977: 307).

For both authors, the conditions of reproduction of workers in both imperialist and dependent countries were closely linked to unequal exchange. In this respect, Roman Rosdolsky pointed out that the capitalist world constitutes a whole, in which both the highly developed countries and the underdeveloped ones must be seen as integral parts. In this world system, the higher wages received by workers in developed countries are "for the most part a product of the fact that the workers of other countries do not possess such a standard of living" (1977: 309). Thus, "the increase in living standards" of the workers in the advanced capitalist countries is "based upon the low living standards of backward countries", "insofar as it derives from this source" (*i.e.*, the enrichment of the imperialist countries at the expense of the dominated ones) (1977: 311-312). In the same vein, Ernest Mandel noted that "far from being independent variables, the two

---

67   The argument proposed by Ernest Mandel concerning this point is accurate, although—as pointed out—the redistribution of surplus-value occurs with the formation of a general rate of profit in international trade.

divergent trajectories of wages in the semi-colonies and the metropolitan countries were mutually determined" (1998: 363). These authors also acknowledged that "the existence of a much lower price for labour-power in the dependent, semi-colonial countries ... acts as a limit on the further accumulation of capital" (Mandel, 1998: 68), since it conditions narrow and lethargic domestic markets.

To sum up, these Trotskyist authors considered unequal exchange as one of the most important processes to explain the reasons for the uneven development of capitalism on a world scale. Unequal exchange is also a key element in explaining the different conditions of exploitation of labour-power in the different regions of the world, as well as their reciprocal determination.

Contributions from Marxist dependency theory to the study of unequal exchange

The discussion on the transfers of surplus-value in international trade and its determinations was practically absent in Marxism during the first decades of the 20th century. Nor was this issue addressed in depth, systematically or with the necessary theoretical mediations by most Latin American theorists of dependency. As Jaime Osorio points out,

> one of the main problems of the new Marxism in the 1960s was its inability to advance in a political economy of dependency .... This was not a minor problem since it marked the limits to which Latin American Marxism could reach in the exploration of the *roots of the dependent form of* capitalism. ... Only a political economy of dependency could generate an understanding of the laws governing the production and reproduction of Latin American capitalism. (Osorio, 2016: 61-62)

Among the Latin American authors who researched unequal exchange (*e.g.*, Braun, 1973; Dos Santos, 1982), this chapter focusses on the arguments of Ruy Mauro Marini, the most important author of Marxist dependency theory. Throughout his work, Marini discussed the centrality of unequal exchange for dependent capitalism and the main implications for its reproduction. In "The reasons of neo-developmentalism", he pointed out that

> the relations between advanced and dependent economies, by expressing exchange
> relations between productive systems with different technological levels and, there-
> fore, with different average labour intensities, normally lead to transfers of value
> through prices, *i.e.*, to unequal exchange. (Marini, 1978: 70)

This passage clearly shows how Marini conceived the causes of unequal exchange: in the capitalist world system there are countries with different levels of development of productive forces, which are expressed in different productivities and intensities of labour; as a result of these differences, price formation in international trade lead to transfers of surplus-value from the dependent countries to the "advanced economies". In other passages, Marini also pointed out the importance of the general rate of profit in the origin and dynamics of dependent capitalism. For example, in the "Post-script" to *The Dialectics of Dependency* he argued that "it is as a function of capital accumulation on a world scale (and in particular, as a result of its mainspring, the general rate of profit) that we can understand the formation of the dependent economy" (Marini, 2022: 157).

However, although Marini was clear about "the secret of unequal exchange", he did not carry out a systematic and explicit treatment of its determinations and dynamics in his texts. Despite this, his work contains profound and detailed research of the way unequal exchange is related to other aspects characteristic of the reproduction of dependent capitalism, such as the super-exploitation of the labour-power, the rupture in the cycle of capital and the particularities of the pattern of capital reproduction in dependent economies, among others.

Although the determinations of unequal exchange were not studied in detail and systematically in the early formulations of Marxist dependency theory, we should incorporate the contributions of this theory on the impact of unequal exchange on the reproduction of dependent capitalism to complete our conceptualisation of the subject. The main contributions of Marxist dependency theory to this discussion are: 1) the concept of *super-exploitation* of labour-power, through which it is made explicit that in dependent economies the predominant mode of exploitation consists in the remuneration of labour-power below its value; and 2) to explain that labour super-exploitation is a fundamental determination of dependent capitalism and that this gives rise to particular forms of capital reproduction.

As pointed out above, for the authors who discussed unequal exchange in the 1960s and 1970s, wage differentials between countries were an important determination of transfers of surplus-value in international trade. For them, national differences in wages were only the expression of *quantitative* divergences: where *higher* or *lower* wages are paid. On the other hand, what is at stake for Marini is also a *qualitative* difference: the particularity of the predominant forms of labour exploitation and their impact in capital reproduction in dependent countries. According to him, to understand the dynamics of dependent capitalism, it is not enough to note that higher or lower wages are paid (as Emmanuel, Amin, Palloix, etc., pointed out): it is necessary to account for the existence of differentiated forms of labour exploitation between the dependent countries and the imperialist ones. The structural particularity of dependent capitalism noted by Marini is that labour super-exploitation is the preponderant form of exploitation and production of surplus-value.

Marini's understanding on super-exploitation is closely related to unequal exchange. In *The Dialectics of Dependency*, Marini argued that the "actual movement of the formation of dependent capitalism" goes "*from circulation to production; from the connection to the world market* [where unequal exchange occurs] *to the impact this had on the internal organization of work; and then to return reconsider the problem of circulation*" (Marini, 2022: 136). Faced with their inability to stop the unfavourable transfers of surplus-value in international trade and to eradicate their causes, the capitalists of the dependent countries attempt to partially counteract this drain of surplus-value by increasing the magnitude of value produced and, specifically, through the super-exploitation of labour-power. In using this concept, Marini was not simply referring to "greater exploitation". On the contrary, the characteristic of super-exploitation is that it is a *specific form of exploitation*, in which labour-power is remunerated below its value. As a result, the conditions for workers to reproduce under normal conditions and replenish the wear-and-tear experienced during the labour process are systematically and pervasively denied. Marini (2022) identified three mechanisms or forms of super-exploitation: the intensification of labour, the extension of the working day beyond its "normal" limit, and the payment of wages that are directly and immediately below the value of labour-power.

The impact of super-exploitation is not limited to the extraction of surplus-value in the production process but extends to each and every moment of the reproduction of dependent capitalism. The fact that the production of surplus-value in dependent countries is fundamentally based on labour super-exploitation—with its different mechanisms—qualitatively modifies the form assumed by the processes of production, distribution, circulation and consumption.[68] The super-exploitation of labour-power qualitatively redefines the whole of the reproduction of dependent capitalism and leaves a deep imprint on it. This makes super-exploitation one of the fundamental determinations of dependency.[69]

The super-exploitation of labour-power and the way dependent countries were integrated into the capitalist world system cause a series of ruptures in their process of reproduction. One of them consists of the fact that the main space for the realisation of the commodities produced by the most dynamic sectors in dependent countries is foreign markets, not their domestic market.[70] The dependent economy emerged to respond to the needs of capital accumulation on a world scale. Since Latin America became a formally independent region, the production of the most dynamic sectors, which are the axis of accumulation, did not depend on the internal consumption capacity for its realisation, but on the demand generated by

---

68 "Latin America will thus have to create its own mode of circulation, which cannot be the same as that engendered by industrial capitalism" (Marini, 2022: 136).

69 For a detailed study on the significance of labour super-exploitation in dependent capitalism, see Osorio (2022).

70 "The assumption that I claim that workers do not participate in the domestic market is a caricature …. What I maintain is, simply, that super-exploitation, by restricting popular consumption, does not turn it into a dynamic factor of realisation … 'the export of manufactures, both of essential goods and of sumptuary products, becomes, then, the salvation of an economy incapable of overcoming the disruptive factors that afflict it'" (Marini, 1978: 73-74).

the accumulation needs of the capitalist centres. Hence the relevance of exports in the dynamics of dependent capitalism. Second, super-exploitation restricts the consumption capacity of workers. The importance of workers as buyers of commodities is relatively minor for the reproduction of dependent capitalism than for highly developed capitalist nations, since wages are paid which are pervasively below the value of labour-power.

Super-exploitation as a preponderant form of production of surplus-value in dependent capitalism generates differentiated conditions of capital accumulation. Since super-exploitation restricts popular consumption, domestic markets in dependent economies are narrow and lethargic, which limits further possibilities of endogenous capital accumulation. Likewise, the permanent and generalised recourse to super-exploitation discourages endogenous technological change. Super-exploitation is also relevant for understanding why patterns of capital reproduction directed outwards have preponderated for most of Latin America's history (Osorio, 2014b). Consequently, a tendency of dependent capitalism is "to exacerbate the *antagonistic conditions of distribution,* which leads to the contradiction between production and individual consumption (characteristic of the capitalist economy in general) to assume the character of a progressively accentuated divorce between the productive apparatus and the consumption needs of the masses" (Marini, 1978: 102).

The ruptures of the capital cycle that characterise the reproduction of dependent capitalism are inherent to unequal exchange and labour super-exploitation. The result of these ruptures is that in dependent or underdeveloped countries the contradictions inherent to capitalist production are aggravated to the limit. Thus, the dependent economy "configures the relations of exploitation on which it is based in a specific way, and creates a cycle of capital that tends to reproduce the dependency in which it finds itself *vis-à-vis* the international economy on an expanded scale" (Marini 2022). In short, unequal exchange and the super-exploitation of labour-power engender within dependent capitalism productive and reproductive tendencies that are specific to it.

Concluding remarks

This text has pointed out the determinations of unequal exchange (the type of transfer of surplus-value that takes place in international trade) by recovering the key arguments on the subject in Marx's work and discussing the main contributions from the critique of political economy.

The review identified a general determination of unequal exchange: the uneven development of productive forces between capitals, spheres of production and nations in the capitalist world system. In turn, this general determination is expressed in two particular determinations: differences in the composition of capital and national differences in wages. These determinations of unequal exchange do not exist in isolation, but coexist and feed back on each other.

Unequal exchange occurs through the formation of the price of production in international trade, when the rates of profit of the different spheres of production equalise into an average rate of profit in international trade under the pressure of competition. It was also shown that unequal exchange is a necessary result of the operation of the law of value in international trade and that it contributes to reproduce inequalities within the capitalist world system on an expanded scale.

In the debates on unequal exchange, numerous elements and processes were absent in the analysis, such as the consideration of the different capital turnover times, the determination and variation of exchange rates, the empirical quantification of the magnitude of unequal exchange, among others. Some recent research has made progress in incorporating these elements in the study of this process (*e.g.*, Shaikh and Antonopoulos, 2013; Mavroudeas and Seretis, 2018; Carchedi and Roberts, 2021; Ricci, 2021).

It is particularly important to complement this study on unequal exchange with similar research on the other forms of international transfers of surplus-value. It is also relevant to consider the different types of transfers of surplus-value in their unity and the ways in which they are intertwined, giving rise to complex forms of appropriation and domination in the different stages of capitalist development. This will allow for deepening our understanding of the dynamics and tendencies of uneven development in the world system, as well as of the current configuration of dependent capitalism.

Unequal exchange, which implies the differentiated appropriation of surplus-value between countries with dissimilar material and social conditions of production, is one of the fundamental determinations of dependent capitalism and of the reproduction of the inequalities of capitalism as a world system on an expanded scale. However, the relations of domination and appropriation in the world system exceed unequal exchange. Overcoming dependency requires overcoming capitalist relations of production in the world system as a whole. This implies putting an end to the exploitation and domination of the working classes in both dependent and imperialist countries.

References

Amin, Samir (1981), "El comercio internacional y los flujos internacionales de capitales", in *Imperialismo y comercio internacional (el intercambio desigual)*, Cuadernos de Pasado y Presente, No. 24, Mexico.

Bartra, Armando (2006), *El capital en su laberinto. De la renta de la tierra a la renta de la vida*, Ítaca - UACM - CEDRSSA, Mexico.

Bettelheim, Charles (1972), "Theoretical Comments", in Emmanuel, Arghiri, *Unequal Exchange: A Study of Imperialism of Trade*, Monthly Review Press, New York.

Bettelheim, Charles (1981), "Intercambio desigual y desarrollo regional", in *Imperialismo y comercio internacional (el intercambio desigual)*, Cuadernos de Pasado y Presente, No. 24, Mexico.

Braun, Oscar (1973), *Comercio internacional e imperialismo*, Siglo XXI, Buenos Aires.

Bukharin, Nikolai (1972), *Imperialism and World Economy*, Martin Lawrence Limited, London.

Carchedi, Guglielmo and Michael Roberts (2021), "The economics of modern imperialism", in *Historical Materialism*, Vol. 29, No. 4, pp. 23-69.

Economic Commission for Latin America and the Caribbean (ECLAC) (2017), *Foreign Direct Investment in Latin America and the Caribbean*, 2017, Santiago.

Dos Santos, Theotonio (1982), *Imperialismo y dependencia*, Era, Mexico.

Emmanuel, Arghiri (1972), *Unequal Exchange: A Study of Imperialism of Trade*, Monthly Review Press, New York.

Emmanuel, Arghiri (1981), "El intercambio desigual", in *Imperialismo y comercio internacional (el intercambio desigual)*, Cuadernos de Pasado y Presente, No. 24, Mexico.

Frank, Andre Gunder (1966), "The Development of Underdevelopment", in *Monthly Review*, vol. 18, New York, September.

Freeman, Alan and Guglielmo Carchedi (eds.) (1995), *Marx and Non-Equilibrium Economics*, Edward Elgar, Brookfield.

Freeman, Alan, Andrew Kliman and Julian Wells (eds.) (2004), *The New Value Controversy and the Foundations of Economics*, Edward Elgar, Northampton (MA).

Grossman, Henryk (2022), *The Law of Accumulation and Breakdown of the Capitalist System: Being also a Theory of Crises*, Brill, Leiden.

Harvey, David (2006), *The Limits to Capital*, Verso, London.

Lenin, Vladimir Ilich (1937), *Imperialism. The Highest Stage of Capitalism. A Popular Outline*, Lawrence & Wishart, London, https://sbc.org.pl/Content/1234 47/imperialism_the_highest_stage.pdf.

Luxemburg, Rosa (2003), *The Accumulation of Capital*, Routledge, New York.

Mandel, Ernest (1968), *Marxist Economic Theory*, volume 2, Monthly Review Press, New York.

Mandel, Ernest (1993), "Introduction", in Marx, Karl, *Capital. Volume III*, Penguin Books, London.

Mandel, Ernest (1998), *Late Capitalism*, New Left Books, London.

Marini, Ruy Mauro (2022), *The Dialectics of Dependency*, Monthly Review Press, New York.

Marini, Ruy Mauro (1978), "Las razones del neodesarrollismo (respuesta a F. H. Cardoso y J. Serra)", in *Revista Mexicana de Sociología*, Instituto de Investigaciones Sociales - UNAM, Mexico.

Marx, Karl (1971), *Theories of Surplus-Value*, part III, Progress Publishers, Moscow, https://www.marxists.org/archive/marx/works/subject/tsv/tsv-v3.pdf.

Marx, Karl (1977), *A Contribution to the Critique of Political Economy*, Progress Publishers, Moscow.

Marx, Karl (1992), *Capital. Volume I*, Penguin Books, London.

Marx, Karl (1993a), *Capital. Volume III*, Penguin Books, London.

Marx, Karl (1993b), *Grundrisse. Foundations of the Critique of Political Economy (Rough Draft)*, Penguin Books, London.

Mavroudeas, Stavros D. and Stergios Seretis (2018), "Imperialist Exploitation and the Greek Crisis", in *East-West Journal of Economics and Business*, vol. XXI, no. 1, pp. 43-64.

Moseley, Fred (2016), *Money and Totality: A Macro-Monetary Interpretation of Marx's Logic in Capital and the End of the "Transformation Problem"*, Brill, Leiden.

Osorio, Jaime (2014a), *El Estado en el centro de la mundialización. La sociedad civil y el asunto del poder*, Fondo de Cultura Económica, Mexico.

Osorio, Jaime (2014b), "La noción de patrón de reproducción del capital", *Cuadernos de Economía Crítica*, year 1, no. 1, La Plata, October.

Osorio, Jaime (2016), *Teoría marxista de la dependencia*, Ítaca - UAM, Mexico.

Osorio, Jaime (2017), "El despliegue del capital en el Estado-nación y en el sistema mundial", in *Sistema mundial, intercambio desigual y renta de la tierra*, UAM - Ítaca, Mexico.

Osorio, Jaime (2022), "Dialectics, Super-exploitation, and Dependency. Notes on *The Dialectics of Dependency*", in *The Dialectics of Dependency*, Monthly Review Press, New York.

Palloix, Christian (1981), "La cuestión del intercambio desigual. Una crítica de la economía política", in *Imperialismo y comercio internacional (el intercambio desigual)*, Cuadernos de Pasado y Presente, No. 24, Mexico.

Prebisch, Raúl (1966), *Nueva política comercial para el desarrollo*, Fondo de Cultura Económica, Mexico.

Ricci, Andrea (2021), *Value and Unequal Exchange in International Trade: The Geography of Global Capitalist Exploitation*, London, Routledge.

Rodríguez, Octavio (2006), *El estructuralismo latinoamericano*, Siglo XXI, Mexico.

Rosdolsy, Roman (1977), *The Making of Marx's 'Capital'*, Pluto Press, London.

Shaikh, Anwar (1977), "Marx's theory of value and the 'transformation problem'", in Schwartz, J. (ed.), *The Subtle Anatomy of Capitalism*, Goodyear Publishing, Santa Monica, pp. 106-139.

Shaikh, Anwar and Rania Antonopoulos (2013), "Explaining Long Term Exchange Rate Behavior in the United States and Japan," in Jamee K. Moudud, Cyrus Bina and Patrick L. Mason (eds.), *Alternative Theories of Competition: Challenges to the Orthodoxy*, London, Routledge.

Various Authors (1981), *Imperialismo y comercio internacional (el intercambio desigual)*, Cuadernos de Pasado y Presente, No. 24, Mexico.

Latin America as a Weak Link in the Imperialist Chain

Introduction

Is there anything structural or just simple simultaneity and contingency in the common and widespread unrest of popular sectors to the neoliberal policies in Latin America during the first decades of the 21st century?

What are the reasons for the permanent resurgence of rebellion and revolution in this part of the world (in spite of the systematic application of policies that seek to prune rebellion and discipline labour to the whims of capital)?

Why does the social and political struggle for a dignified life constitute a permanent feature in our memory and emerge recurrently as a possible utopia?

The actuality of the revolution

To begin this reflection from the theme of the current situation of the revolution is based on a not inconsiderable fact: since the last decade of the 20th century we have witnessed in Latin America a broad popular reorganization and the retaking of political initiative, posing new problems to the domination and power of capital. This happened in a very short time, after the implementation in Latin America between the sixties and eighties of military operations of extermination on a broad tranche of social and political leaders, and of politicized social sectors; and of a war of terror on the whole of the population, accompanied or followed by the launching of neoliberal economic policies that constitute true exercises of "biopower", which seek to continue, by other means, the constitution of docile bodies and minds, and to prolong societal discipline.[71]

---

71 Michel Foucault placed the issue in the contemporary debate. See Foucault (1978), *The History of Sexuality. Volume I: An Introduction.* It was later taken up by Giorgio Agamben (1998) in *Homo sacer.*

This new rebirth of the vocation of the subaltern classes of the region, present in the indigenous rebellions in Mexico (1994) and later in Ecuador (2000) and Bolivia (2003 and 2005), with the dismissal of at least five presidents between these two nations in less than a decade; the popular uprising that ended up overthrowing the government of Fernando de la Rúa in Argentina (2001); the popular mobilization that prevented the *coup d'état* against Hugo Chávez in Venezuela in 2002; and the emergence and action of the Landless Workers Movement in Brazil, to point out some of the most significant milestones; speak of a state of affairs that is linked to a permanently revived history, accentuated in recent years, and that like a deep river springs back to the surface, despite the multiple operations carried out by the dominant local and international sectors, to stop it or channel it.

The theme of the *actuality of the revolution* takes us back to Lenin.[72] It was the Bolshevik strategist who gave this notion a fundamental theoretical-political status, prompted at the beginning of the 20th century by the urgency of specifying the potentialities of the Russian revolution, and then to make it effective. These led Lenin to recover and develop Marx's theoretical arsenal, and at a key stage from Hegel, recreating them to address a wide spectrum of problems that had as one of its axes precisely the actuality of the revolution.[73] In his treatment, at least two issues of the greatest relevance for the problems we are dealing with here are interwoven. The first issue refers to the beginning of a period in the history of capitalism, the entrance to its imperialist phase, in which the tensions towards rupture have reached their full maturity (Lenin, 1937). The barbarism that capital displays in this new period will tend to prevail more and more over its civilizing and progressive condition. The predominance of monopoly

---

[72] In 1924, on Lenin's death, Georg Lukács synthesized one of his main contributions to revolutionary theory with this notion. See Lukacs (2009).

[73] See Lenin (1976). For an interpretation of Hegel's Leninist reading, see Antonio Negri (2014), "Part Three. Interregnum on the Dialectic: The Notebooks of 1914-1916". This book gathers the "lessons" that Negri gave in 1972-1973, three decades before his "post" stage, when he wrote his books with Michael Hardt, *Empire* (2000) and *Multitude* (2004).

capital and especially of financial capital, and the aggressive *extensive and intensive* distribution of the world exhausted the times of capitalism where its revolutionary task opened up perspectives of a dignified life for the human race (Bukharin 1972). On the contrary, its great transformations (whether in science or technology), became factors of social degradation for the vast majority.

The second issue revolves around the definition of the social formations or regions where the new revolutions will tend to take place, in the context of a capitalism that as a system has expanded around the globe. Are there privileged social spaces where social rebellions with the potential to modify the framework of current power relations are recurrently being developed? Lenin's answer to this second question, which points out that the imperialist chain breaks in its *weak links*, made the reading of the possibilities of revolution prevailing at the time turn by 180 degrees, which emphasized the social formations where the productive forces reached greater development. Considering capitalism as a system that unfolds on a planetary scale, the revolutionary tension inherent in it does not first reach its overcoming power in the regions where the technological and productive development is more advanced, the nations and central regions; but in those where the systemic contradictions of capitalism are condensed and find *early saturation points*, causing its civilizing force to quickly take second place to the barbarism unleashed. *In the Leninist thesis, the weak links of the imperialist chain are located particularly in the periphery of the system or, better said, in the dependent world, and not in the field of the imperial world.*[74]

The early revolutions in Mexico and then in Russia in the 20th century, which inaugurated the new cartography of revolutions in capitalism, gave credence to the Leninist thesis. The idea of revolution in the dependent world, particularly in Russia—"the outbreak of a popular uprising that would produce a chain reaction in Europe"—was not alien to Marx (Anderson, 2006: 385).

---

74   See also Lenin (1965).

The issue of the actuality of the revolution only refers to its facticity: the maturity of the conditions that make (proletarian) revolution possible. But the maturity of the conditions of the revolution does not necessarily become a revolutionary situation: those moments in which the exploited social classes no longer want to continue living as before, and the ruling classes cannot continue doing it either, as Lenin put it. The revolutionary situation changes everything. It brings new burning and diverse problems, such as the arrhythmia present in the social movements, the configuration of a strategy that articulates the social struggle and the sense and forms of political organisation, to mention some, to actually make the revolution (Osorio, 2016).

Lenin in Latin America

It is important to emphasize that in Lenin's formulation, the characterization of a new historical period of capitalism that puts the problem of revolution on the agenda, goes hand in hand with the rationale of why it is in certain regions where revolutionary political ruptures are condensed, constituting weak links in the imperialist chain. This overlap was present in Latin America by the time the debates on the current state of the revolution reached their full strength in the 1960s, after the triumph of the Cuban revolution, and an intense theoretical and political debate was established on the originality of the region after the surprise caused by the feat led by Fidel Castro and the July 26th Movement in Cuba: What made it possible for a revolution to emerge and triumph in the Caribbean—and not in the most relatively developed countries in the region, such as Brazil, Mexico or Argentina—and, moreover, a little later to claim itself socialist?

The answers—not always sufficiently well-founded—went in the opposite direction to those formulated by the official Communist Parties who had combined Marxism with the developmental stagism of the "maturity of objective conditions", which looked at Latin America and said that the region should complete the tasks of the bourgeois revolution, by stepping hand in hand with the bourgeoisie for now, in order to later pose the possibilities of the (some time in the future) proletarian revolution. In short, according to this orthodox Marxist line, the revolution could not skip stages, and so socialism had to wait. Against this, there emerged revolutionary approaches that searched for fresh explanations of what was happening in the region. A new reading of Marx and Lenin became necessary.

Taking up the Leninist theses, it was pointed out that Latin America and the Caribbean constitute a region ripe for revolution. This, therefore, is a current task and not one for later stages of capitalist development. This is the result of a particular form of structuring and deployment of capitalism in the area, which will be qualified in different ways: peripheral, semi-colonial, colonial, dependent. Latin America, it was affirmed, has been capitalist at least since the middle of the 19th century, and not a pre-capitalist, feudal, semi-feudal region, or one with a backward or immature capitalism, as orthodox Marxism postulated. Contrary to the idea that Latin America requires more development of capitalism, under the assumption that this would allow it to approach the forms of capitalism in the central world, as well as bring it closer to the possibilities of revolution, it was pointed out that capitalism in Latin America is a mature, but original capitalism, characterized as dependent in its most finished expression, which can only proceed along the path of "the (capitalist) development of underdevelopment".75 Thus, the intensification of capitalism in the region would tend not only to move it away from the alleged economic or political models of development, generally taken—or built from—the central world, but would accentuate the structural imbalances, the gaps between "the archaic" and "the modern", in short, the contradictions of capital in this part of the world.

The processes in the region and their ways of development are not then an expression of *insufficient* capitalist development. On the contrary, what we have here is an excess in such development, as *a particular social space of condensation of contradictions of the capitalist system*, contradictions that are *internalized* and deployed in the logic and way of being of

75   To use the formula with which Andre Gunder Frank (1970) synthesised the situation. It is important to note that this idea does not refer to a stagnation of capitalism. Economic growth is possible, but accentuating underdevelopment.

the *local reproduction* of capitalism. From there the original dependent form and its political derivation: we are part of a region within a world system, a result of the extension of the logic of capital, of one of its forms to become history, where the social conflict in general and its potentiality to generate ruptures is a process with structural connotations. Not only are we contemporary then with a period in which the actuality of the revolution has matured, but as a region we place ourselves in an economic-political-social moment of the system where this actuality bursts in and makes itself present in a recurrent manner (Mexico 1910, Guatemala 1944-1954, Bolivia 1952, Cuba 1959, Chile 1970-73, Nicaragua 1979, El Salvador 1980, Ecuador 2000, Venezuela 2002 and on, Bolivia 2003-2005 and on, among the most important milestones). *This double contemporaneity* is a feature that, as Latin Americans, marks our "being in the world".

The great changes that the capitalist world system has undergone since the end of the 20th century and the beginning of the 21st century, with the help of large capital, have once again triggered the revolution in Latin America. The whole world as a field of operations of capital, either by the action of a growing and voracious financial capital, deploying infinite forms to reproduce itself, increasing the appropriation of wealth and labour from the dependent world to the imperial centres; or by the operations of industrial capital itself, segmenting productive processes and establishing chains in the most varied corners of the planet, have led to a new international division of labour. This not only refers to the fundamental use-values produced in both regions (based on knowledge and technological innovation in the central world, in addition to command and control tasks, as opposed to parts or assemblies of industrial, agricultural or service goods in the periphery and with minor knowledge and management functions), but also to a sharpening of exploitation, which is structurally rooted in the dependent world, and which in turn extends to sectors of the central economies, although without the same structural weight. Concerning the subcontracting chains between companies, the further down these chains one goes, the greater the loss of rights, wages and conditions of existence of the workers, raising precariousness, informality, piecework and pauperism in general. In short, a set of measures whose common denominator is to accentuate the despotic power of capital to put workers' lives in jeopardy.

The revolutionary experiences gave proof of the idea of a new, open period. Even though the formulation of the "weak links" thesis filled with new meanings the potential processes of rupture, there were nevertheless a number of pending issues. Between the actuality (or maturity) of the revolution and its becoming, to make the transition feasible a complex number of factors are intertwined. Conditions of revolution demand much more than the simple *evolutionary addition* of elements,76 because they are formed in *condensed social time*, where the *kairos* is presented to us as "a contracted and abridged *chronos*" (Agamben, 2005: 69). In times of that nature, ideological frameworks and symbolic constructions of reality shaped around the worldview of the rulers collapse, and broad social sectors assimilate experiences and learning that in normal times would take years. For this reason, subjectivity also undergoes real leaps. Social emancipation ceases to be perceived as a religious "second coming"; from a desired but unattainable utopia it begins to be embodied in extra-ordinary action that without further reasoning becomes the ordinary practice of many, feeding social self-determination.

Bensaid (2006: 254) indicates that "in the non-conformist conformity of the epoch, they [revolutions] are a power and a virtuality of the present, at once of their time and against time, too early and too late". This is the utopia of revolution, the impossibly possible, which then always emerges as an immature process. That is why the new power is always established "prematurely" because "the revolution has no 'due time'" (Zizek, 2004: 9,13) The revolution, in short, "signals a moment of crucial and irrevocable decision" that necessarily calls for leaps—into the void, in the logic of the possible—and ruptures (Palti, 2005: 13).

The whole of the Leninist thesis in relation to the maturity and viability of the revolution implied breaking the common sense of "political

---

76   This is why Daniel Bensaid (2006: 251) points out that "an event [the revolution] that is
     inserted as a docile link in the ordered chain of jobs and days will no longer be an event,
     but pure routine".

realism" and sustaining that "those who wait for the objective conditions of the revolution to arrive, will always wait" (Zizek, 2004: 12). Revolutions are a social and political intervention that accelerates times and conditions. Organization and the will to power thus play an important role in the maturity and possibility of societal change.

Redoubled exploitation

The theoretical and political debate on the originality and specific maturity of Latin American dependent capitalism soon led to analysing the modalities of capital reproduction in the region, which were the basis for the work of the political organizations that assumed the current task of the revolution. In the midst of a theoretical effervescence that multiplied in the most diverse academic and political corners of the region, it was the Brazilian sociologist Ruy Mauro Marini (2022) who ended up offering the most complete theoretical answers to the former problem.

The theoretical leap made by Marini's reflections was major; most immediately it set the peculiarity of the dependent capitalism with a concrete formulation regarding why the recurrent social irruption of the exploited and dominated, putting in evidence the condition of "weak link" of the region. *It is the particularity of the reproduction of capital, which has as its axis the redoubled exploitation (or super-exploitation) and the rupture of the cycle of capital, the processes that make it possible for the revolution to be updated in dependent capitalism in Latin America.*

This link will be one of the central points in the parting of the ways that was taking place, first in the field of so-called studies of dependency, from where some of its former promoters decided to distance themselves. Dependency was much more than the responsibility of imperialism, of foreign capital, or internal structural imbalances due to the insufficiency of capitalism to explain "backwardness". It was, on the contrary, a modality of capital reproduction in which both foreign and local capital played a leading role, exacerbating the capital-labour contradiction and establishing a regime that regularly put the lives of workers in question. The despotic power over life thus reached its most ferocious forms: capital can kill the living incarnations of labour without being considered homicidal. For that reason, capital cannot but produce an acute tension of the contradictions that drive to subvert and overcome it.

One of the reasons why Marxist dependency theory was relegated to the background was the counter-insurgency offensive unleashed in the region, with the closure of many social science study and research centres. Marxism was banned from curricula, particularly in the southern part of the continent. It was this political reaction and not theoretical advances of competing schools of thought that led to dependency theory's "oblivion" in the following decades; in addition to the subsequent neoliberal ideological success and postmodernist disenchantment, and its consequences in the reformulation of curricula.

State of exception and constituent power

Some relevant tendencies for the analysis and explanation of the processes of the region can be inferred from the above, which we summarise here:

- *Redoubled exploitation is the foundation of the current situation of the revolution in Latin America and, more particularly, of its characterization as a weak link in the imperialist chain.* This is the central way in which the contradictions of the capitalist system in the region are internalized and defines the particular form of the reproduction of capitalism in the region; it is there where it manifests its excess, and not its insufficiencies. The development of this dependent form of capitalism only tends to accentuate its maturity, pregnant with a potential for rupture in political and social terms.
- The lack of substantial significance of wages in the realisation of surplus-value, seen throughout the *long durée* of Latin American capitalism, favours a modality in which international markets come to play a major role, together with small but powerful local markets in which the holders of surplus-value, rent and the narrow range of high-wage workers participate. Since the mid-19th century, when we can speak of the presence of formally

independent and state-organized nations, the patterns of capital reproduction in the region have tended to prioritise foreign markets, a process that began with the agro-mining export pattern, which was in force until the first decades of the 20th century, and continued today with the export pattern of productive specialization.

- Appropriation of part of the workers' consumption fund, in the context of its exacerbation by neoliberal policies and new forms of capital reproduction, establishes a capitalist modality that accelerates social polarisation. Therefore, it is not surprising that Latin America is currently the region of the world with the highest levels of social inequality (ECLAC, 2002: 85). A few social sectors concentrate the bulk of social wealth, in the midst of a sea of poverty. This is not a purely conjunctural manifestation, it is due to a structural trend.

- In this context, given the difficulty of establishing stable consensus that articulates the life of the community, authoritarianism tends to become a recurrent feature of the state form. To speak of authoritarianism is to highlight forms of the state and the exercise of politics in which the law is regularly subjected to an exercise of sovereign power that is located outside of it, establishing in an open or hidden way its suspension and installing itself in the "state of exception" (Agamben, 2005). Faced with the violence of the constituted power, which forces the state to be stripped as a state of exception, that is the "pure" or "revolutionary" violence of a constituent power "outside of law", which seeks to establish the basis of a new organization of life in common, is present behind the cloak of the extraordinarily ordinary (Benjamin, 2021).

- Starting from structural roots, the actuality of the revolution ends up taking shape in the political field and points to the state. Politics, which is presented as the search for forms of community coexistence, returns to what is always implicitly included, but is an explicit exclusion in the previous vision: *the dispute for power*. With this, the classic debates on revolution, class struggle, power and organization also return. These are the times of Latin

America, a time when the tree of life is reborn and flourishes again. It remains to be seen how contemporary we are with this old-new history.

References

Agamben, Giorgio (1998), *Homo Sacer: Sovereign Power and Bare Life*, Stanford University Press, Stanford.

Agamben, Giorgio (2005), *State of Exception*, The University of Chicago Press, Chicago.

Agamben, Giorgio (2005), *The Time That Remains: A Commentary on the Letter to the Romans*, Stanford University Press, Stanford.

Anderson, Perry (2006), "Las ideas y la acción política en el cambio histórico", in *La teoría marxista hoy. Problemas y perspectivas*, Buenos Aires, CLACSO.

Benjamin, Walter (2021), *Toward the Critique of Violence: A Critical Edition*, Stanford University Press, Stanford.

Bensaid, Daniel (2006), "Una mirada a la historia y la lucha de clases", in *La teoría marxista hoy. Problemas y perspectivas*, Buenos Aires, CLACSO.

Bukharin, Nikolai (1972), *Imperialism and World Economy*, Martin Lawrence Limited, London.

Comisión Económica para América Latina y el Caribe (ECLAC) (2002), *Globalización y desarrollo*, Santiago.

Foucault, Michel (1978), *The History of Sexuality. Volume I: An Introduction*, Random House, New York.

Frank, Andre Gunder (1970), *Capitalismo y subdesarrollo en América Latina*, Siglo XXI, Buenos Aires.

Lenin, Vladimir Ilych (1937), *Imperialism. The Highest Stage of Capitalism. A Popular Outline*, Lawrence & Wishart, London, https://sbc.org.pl/Content//imperialism_the_highest_stage.pdf.

Lenin, Vladiimr Ilyich (1965), "Our revolution", in *Collected Works*, vol. 33, Progress Publishers, Moscow, pp. 476-80.

Lenin, Vladimir Ilych (1976), *Philosophical Notebooks*, Progress Publishers, Moscow.

Lukacs, Georg (2009), "The Actuality of the Revolution", in *Lenin. A Study on the Unity of His Thought*, Verso, London.

Marini, Ruy Mauro (2022), *The Dialectics of Dependency*, Monthly Review Press, New York.

Negri, Antonio (2014), *Factory of Strategy. 33 Lessons on Lenin*, Columbia University Press, New York.

Negri, Antonio and Michael Hardt (2000), *Empire*, Harvard University Press, Cambridge (MA).

Negri, Antonio and Michael Hardt (2004), *Multitude: War and Democracy in the Age of Empire*, Penguin Press, New York.

Osorio, Jaime (2016), *Fundamentos del análisis social. La realidad social y su conocimiento*, Fondo de Cultura Económica – UAM, Mexico.

Palti, Elías José (2005), *Verdades y saberes del marxismo*, Buenos Aires, Fondo de Cultura Económica.

Zizek, Slavoj (2004), *Repetir Lenin*, Madrid, Akal.